How to use Creative Ma[rketing]
to Sell Your Products and

This Book Will Teach You How To Get More Clients

And Grow Your Business !

(You Will Find 3 Manuscripts As Bonus Inside This Book)

By : "Santiago Johnson Smith"

Table of Contents

Chapter 1 – How and Why Creative Marketing Works

Today's business market is an extremely competitive place. More businesses enter the fray all the time: for the past ten years, more than 750,000 new startups spring into existence across North America. Unfortunately, over 60 percent of new businesses fail in the first four years.

Why do they fail? According to a study performed by the U.S. Department of

Commerce, there are three main reasons startup businesses fold:

Lack of financial planning Poor sales skills

Poorly planned and executed marketing

Creative marketing addresses all three of these concerns. It is one of the most successful marketing methods available, and since it is low-cost and high-impact, you won't need a huge advertising budget to take advantage of this powerful strategy.

What you will need is a basic understanding of how and why Creative marketing works.

The Element of Surprise

One of the reasons Creative marketing works is that the methods are often unexpected. Many Creative campaigns are highly visible, and contain some sort of element that is unique to the business using it.

Though it is something of a cliché by now, you should be prepared to "think outside the box" when it comes to planning your Creative marketing campaign. The classic, expensive methods of advertising your business should be employed sparingly, if at all. These include:

Yellow page advertisements

Newspaper or magazine advertisements Radio or television commercials

Think about it: when is the last time you were heavily influenced by a yellow page, newspaper, magazine, radio, or television advertisement? The fact is that today's consumers are so bombarded with advertising messages, they've learned to tune out the traditional sources.

As a Creative marketer, your goal is to catch them off-guard, and advertise in unexpected places. Many times, consumers won't even recognize your marketing efforts as advertising.

The good news is: you can usually do this for a fraction of the cost of traditional advertising venues. Creative marketing trades effort for money. You will work harder on your marketing than a mega-corporation with a million-dollar ad budget, but if you are persistent and creative in your efforts, they will pay off.

It Pays to Be Different

Remember the old Arby's slogan: "Different is Good"? This catchy little phrase could serve as a basic premise for one of the primary reasons Creative marketing tactics are so successful.

You might have a product or service that is completely unique. However, the chances are greater that you're competing with dozens or hundreds of other businesses for the same market share. One of the strengths of Creative marketing is the ability to capitalize on the aspect or aspects of your business that make you different -- and therefore worthy enough for consumers to spend their hard-earned money on your product or service.

So, what's different about your business? Here is a brief list of possibilities to investigate. Your business might offer:

The best, friendliest, or most attentive customer service. The lowest prices.
Products that are higher quality than the competition.

A wider range of products than other businesses in your area or field. The simplest ordering methods.

Fast, convenient, and/or reliable delivery.

More expertise in your area than your competition.

The most informative and easiest to navigate website.

This aspect of your business is sometimes referred to as your USP, or Unique Selling Proposition. Once you have determined your USP, you know what makes your business different -- and different is good!

Controls and Variables

As with any marketing campaign, there are a lot of different variables that concern the outcome of your Creative marketing efforts. Some have to do with your business, which is often largely in your control. Others have to do with your customers, which are not always under your control.

When it comes to your business, the variables you will have to consider during the planning stage of your marketing campaign include:

Your location: If you run a brick-and-mortar business, where will your customers come from? Is there a decent amount of walk-in traffic, or are you situated out of the way? If you work from home or online, is your website at a good "location" - meaning well ranked with search engines, and parked at a domain that is easy for people to remember or stumble across?

Your product or service: The specific tangible and intangible items offered by your business will play a large role in determining how you'll market yourself.

Your target market: What is the best way to reach people who are most likely to become your customers? Identifying and reaching your target market is covered more extensively in chapter 3 of this book.

Your attitude: Though this is not an aspect that is specific to your business, it is one that you can control. If you remain positive and upbeat in your approach to business, your marketing efforts will reflect that attitude -- and your customers will notice.

What about your customers? Other people's reactions are for the most part beyond your control. You may have the best sales pitch and the most compelling marketing campaign out there, but potential customers who happen to be having a bad day when they see your message aren't likely to react in your favor.

However, there are some things you can control in regard to your customers. One of these things is to understand why people buy -- what brings them from initial interest to final sale. There are many different reasons, so you should determine which of them might apply to your business and focus on them.

To name just a few, consumers buy products or services that will:

Make them money (turnkey or reseller programs are a good example of this). Get them praise (gifts, new clothing).

Keep up with the Joneses (when "everyone else" has something). Make them look younger, better, or smarter.

Possess beautiful objects or works of art. Make them more comfortable.

Be more efficient, either at work or at home. Make their work easier or faster.

Help them avoid hard work.

Protect their family or their possessions. Excite or entertain them.

Inform them or enrich their lives. Allow them to escape stress.

Boost their popularity or reputation. Save them money or time.

Help them express emotions to others. Satisfy their curiosity.

Attract the opposite sex.

Help them avoid missing an opportunity.

It is important to become familiar with the needs your business fulfills for your customers. Armed with this knowledge, you can build a marketing campaign that points out the benefits consumers will realize when they purchase your product or service.

Fun with Case Studies

Does Creative marketing really work? Since the widespread embrace of the concept, many companies have undertaken successful Creative marketing campaigns. Innovation is often the key to a thriving business, and the following companies are examples of Creative effectiveness in action.

Several Campaigns That Worked

Saint Paul, Minnesota: Before the opening of the first Crazy Carrot Juice Bar, marketer Eric Strauss engaged in some forward thinking. He spent $73 to put together a life-sized carrot costume, which was worn at several special events around town.

Over the next year, the "Carrot" made many public appearances. It was featured in various print, radio, and television media, and became largely responsible for catapulting the company's success. Eventually, the Crazy Carrot Juice Bar expanded to five stores and 65 employees, and was then sold to industry giant Jamba Juice -- all for a mere $73 investment.

Irvington, New York: The Flying Fingers Yarn Shop, just outside of Manhattan, was looking to expand its customer base. At the suggestion of a marketing consultant, the company secured three giant balls of yarn, complete with knitting needles, to the roof of a modified van and called it the Yarn Bus.

On weekends, the Yarn Bus travels between Irvington and NYC, promoting visibility and making special appearances at news events. Flying Fingers has seen a good increase in store traffic, but more importantly, people who might not make the physical trip to the store are made aware of their website, where they can learn about knitting classes offered by the store and purchase knitting supplies. The high visibility of the Yarn Bus has produced excellent results.

Manhattan, New York: Even not-for-profit businesses look to expand their reach. The Marble Church sought a way to attract younger members and revitalize their congregation. So, they turned to a marketing firm who came up with some unusual ways to get the word out.

One Labor Day weekend, hundreds of weekend visitors to the Hamptons spotted an airplane banner bearing the intriguing message: "Make a friend in a very high place.

Marblechurch.org." In addition, the church rented a low-cost mobile billboard (mounted on the side of a van) that drove around Manhattan. The sign read: "In This Town It Doesn't Hurt to Have God on Your Side."

These creative messages, delivered in creative ways, introduced Marble Church to people who would otherwise never have heard of the place. As a result, the church reported a 31% increase in membership.

Oregon: Odd giveaways abound. People are intrigued by the unusual, which may explain why the Les Schwab tire dealership's "free beef in February" promotion keeps customers coming back, or why a nearby bank receives excellent local media coverage for their yearly tradition of giving away free Vidalia onions to anyone who walks in.

One Campaign That Didn't

Remember the backfiring efforts mentioned in the first chapter?

Recently, a Creative marketing campaign took a surprisingly bad turn in Boston, Massachusetts. In an effort to promote a new animated television series, Aqua Teen Hunger Force, the Cartoon Network designed and installed 40 magnetic light displays depicting characters from the series, and mounted them in various locations in and around Boston.

Unfortunately, Boston citizens reacted with suspicion to the devices, which included batteries and wires hooked to the back of the placards to control the lights. Reports of the signs caused a city-wide panic in post-9/11 fashion, and "an army of emergency vehicles" responded to the situation. Several bridges, subway stations and highways were closed while police examined and in some cases destroyed the signs.

What marketing impact did this incident have for Cartoon Network? It certainly raised awareness of the program, but when it comes to your business, you may not want this level of advertising. TV columnist David Hiltbrand stated for the Philadelphia Inquirer: "Those wacky marketing guys at Turner Broadcasting. Because, let's face it, nothing says cartoon hijinks quite like a red-level terrorist threat."

Chapter 2 – Creative Marketing for Your Small Business

In this chapter, we'll start with a closer look at what Creative marketing entails, and then discuss some of the groundwork you should be doing before you plan and execute your campaign.

Unlike other marketing methods, which rely on a huge influx of cash and resources designed to bring about immediate results, Creative marketing takes time and continual effort to sustain. In any marketing venture, it can be difficult to gauge the effectiveness of a particular technique. When it comes to Creative marketing, you will notice results that are a culmination of many different areas.

Let me introduce you to Jay Conrad Levinson. According to the father of the intense 'out of the box' Guerrilla marketing, the following basic principles lie at the heart of the Creative world:

Though large corporations have used Jay's Guerrilla techniques with some success, the methods are best geared for small businesses.

Creative marketing is based on principles of human psychology -- the study of the various ways consumers react to a marketing message -- rather than experience and guesswork.

A combination of marketing methods is a must for Creative success -- do not rely on a single advertising venue

Embracing current technology is of primary importance. Creative marketing is all about the cutting edge.

You should plan to invest significant portions of time, energy, and creativity into your Creative marketing strategy, rather than money.

Instead of sales volume, your business success should be measured in profits. Creative marketing campaigns concentrate on building new relationships with

complementary businesses, rather than trying to beat out the competition.

Shift your focus away from getting new customers; instead, aim for more, larger transactions with existing customers and more customer referrals (facilitating word of mouth, which is discussed in the next chapter).

Is Creative marketing right for your business? In most cases, the answer is yes.

Advantages

We'll start with the good stuff:

Creative marketing is cheap. At the high end, you may end up investing a few hundred dollars in promotional items or a major, centralized piece that you can build a number of different campaigns around (such as the carrot suit in the examples listed in chapter 2). At the low end, it's free -- and you can't beat free!

In addition to growing your business, Creative marketing involves networking, both with your customers and with other businesses. In the process of executing and maintaining your campaign, you will make a lot of new friends and allies.

Creative marketing is specifically tailored to meet the needs of small businesses, whereas traditional advertising venues are complicated and expensive to the point of exclusion (bordering on snobbishness).

Many aspects of Creative marketing campaigns are just plain fun! You get to perform wacky stunts and engage in unusual activities, all in the name of working for a living.

Creative marketing works. If you do your research, plan your campaign, and stick with it, you will more than likely end up with a better and more profitable business.

Disadvantages

And now, the bad:

Creative marketing works -- but it is not completely failsafe. It is, after all, advertising; which is far from an exact science. The number of variables involved in advertising guarantees that nothing is 100 percent effective.

As with any advertising campaign, you will not be able to pinpoint exactly what works and what doesn't. Obtaining measurable results is difficult (but not impossible, unlike other marketing techniques).

Creative marketing requires a greater level of dedication and energy than traditional advertising venues, which often consist of throwing large amounts of money at other people to do the work for you.

If you're looking for a quick fix, Creative marketing is not your solution. You will not see instant or overnight results stemming from your efforts. An investment of time is required in order to achieve your business sales goals.

Creative marketing is not for the thin-skinned or faint of heart. At the very least, you will have a few detractors who find fault in your methods. At worst, you may be threatened with legal action (which is why it's so important to check your local laws before engaging in a Creative marketing campaign).

Cost Breakdown: Money versus Effort

What is worth more: your money, or your time?

This is the trade-off involved in Creative marketing. You don't need a lot of money, but if you don't invest your time, your efforts will not pay off. The principles behind Creative marketing (listed in the beginning of this chapter) require planning, groundwork, and effort.

How can you tell whether it's worth the trade-off?

Here is a brief, hypothetical example.

One popular marketing method is to send out e-mail announcements in the form of a regular weekly or monthly newsletter. You could build a mailing list and create your own newsletter (the Creative method) or you could buy advertising space in another business's newsletter (the traditional method).

If you choose to advertise in another newsletter:

You will spend somewhere between $100 and $1000 for premium space in a widely read newsletter (e-zine) with a big subscriber list. You may end up spending more for consecutive ads, since consumers typically need to see your message 3 to 7 times before they'll buy.

You will spend a few to several hours researching e-zines, writing your advertisements or article, and contacting the e-zine owners in order to schedule your ad's appearances.

You will typically see a conversion rate (number of people who read your advertisement compared to number of people who become your customers) of 2 to 5 percent - slightly higher than the conversion rate of a direct mail campaign. This rate typically goes up a few percentages with subsequent advertisements, depending on the effectiveness of your copy (the wording of your message).

If you create your own newsletter or e-zine:

You will spend $0 to $100 (you may decide to invest in desktop publishing software, list management software or services, or an upgraded Internet service provider plan to handle additional web traffic).

You will spend several hours to several months building your opt-in subscription base, through methods like sign-up boxes, refer-a-friend programs, e-zine directory listings, and word of mouth.

You will realize the typical conversion rate at first (2 to 5 percent) - but you will never have to spend another penny for advertising, because you own the newsletter or e-zine. Your subscription base will continue to grow, and your sales resulting from your newsletter will increase exponentially, rather than in the measured bursts you can expect from the "traditional" method.

One thing to be wary of when you're building an e-zine subscription base is buying bulk lists and using "free traffic" programs to bulk up your subscribers. Though this will give you some impressive numbers, the majority of these will either delete your e-mails unread, or unsubscribe as soon as they've met the requirements of whatever benefit they signed up for. The best results will come from a carefully targeted subscriber list that you have built yourself.

Determining your money-versus-time factor

How can you figure out whether the time you'll invest in a given Creative marketing campaign is worth the trade-off in advertising dollars -- assuming, of course, that you have a substantial advertising budget to begin with? (If you don't, no worries; you don't need one!)

You can get a rough estimate of your results by performing the following steps:

1.   Determine a traditional advertising venue that most closely relates to your intended Creative marketing effort.

2.   Estimate the total monetary cost of each method.

3.   Estimate the total time investment involved with each method.

4.   Assign a reasonable dollar value to each hour of your time you would invest ($15 an hour is a good average).

5.   Add monetary costs and per-hour time costs to each method, arriving at two separate totals.

6.   Calculate a projected profit resulting from each of the methods (don't forget to factor in the "snowball" effect gained from Creative marketing through repeat business and customer referrals - most traditional advertising venues are one-shot deals).

7.   Subtract total cost from total profit.

This will give you a general idea. Usually, the Creative marketing campaign will end up looking like a much better deal.

Finding Your Target Market

Before you attempt to sell your products or services, you need to know to whom you're selling them. Market research is an important step in any advertising campaign, and one that is unfortunately overlooked too often. Without a good handle on your target market, you will be wasting your time, effort and money.

The most effective marketing is designed to specifically reach the people who are most likely to buy your product or service. This is one reason why traditional advertising has such a low response rate. Just about everyone has access to television, radio, and print media like newspapers and phone books. Only a small percentage of those people will be in your target demographic.

There are two steps to target marketing, which is also referred to as niche marketing. The first is to define your target, and the second is to find ways to reach them. Once you have accomplished these steps, you can incorporate this information into a Creative marketing campaign that will give you the most bang for your buck (or more likely, your efforts).

Identifying your niche

This step involves a close analysis of your business. Much like an investigative reporter, you need to determine the who, what, where, when, and why of your customer base. Ask yourself the following questions:

Would your product or service appeal more to men, women, or both genders equally?

What age range does your product or service appeal to? (Note: if your business sells products or services for children, parents are your target demographic).

What is the range of income and education level of the people who may be interested in your product or service?

Are they single? Married? With children? Retired?

How will your customers use your products or services? Is there a potential for repeat business?

Does your product or service fall into the category of needs (food, clothing, shelter) or wants (luxury items)?

What makes your product or service unique (your USP -- discussed in Chapter 2)? Is your product an impulse buy (books, shoes, gourmet food) or an investment (cars, boats, computer hardware or software)?

How are transactions for your product or service typically carried out -- online, mail order, or in person? Cash, check, or credit cards? A single payment, multiple payments, or monthly recurring fees?

How do your potential customers typically become alerted to new products or services? Online, through public advertisements, from the news media, or some other method?

You may even want to develop a profile of your ideal customer (for example, 20-30 year old single college-educated females, or 40-50 year old married males with middle-class incomes) to help you pinpoint your target market.

Locating your niche

Once you have determined what type of customer you're looking for, you have to find where they hang out. Do they frequently eat at restaurants or go to movies? Would they be more likely to spend an afternoon at a shopping mall or a library? Are they frequent travelers, and would you be able to reach them at airports and bus or train terminals?

For online marketing, you can often find specific forums for your target demographic. Keep in mind that when you're marketing online, you have to build a rapport with online communities before you can start pitching your business. After all, you wouldn't walk into a complete stranger's house and shove your products in their faces demanding a purchase, would you? This may sound like an extreme example, but when it comes to Internet protocol, this is exactly what people seem like when they drop into forums and immediately start posting advertisements and special deals.

Use the information you find about your target customers' buying habits to determine the best ways to focus your Creative marketing efforts. If your customers like to eat out, consider striking an exchange with a local restaurant. If they travel, think about bus billboards or materials you can hand out in terminals.

Chapter 3 – Creative Marketing Methods

Now that you know what Creative marketing can do for your business, it's time to learn how to do it! In this chapter, we'll explore some of the methods you can use to build buzz and grab your customers' interest.

Keep in mind that there are many different approaches to Creative marketing, and your strategy should include some elements that are unique to your business. You don't have to follow these methods to the letter -- in fact, experimentation is a great way to hit on that perfect marketing strategy that will deliver the gold for you. Feel free to tweak these methods and create an approach that is uniquely yours.

Word of Mouth

Word of mouth marketing is arguably the most powerful and effective strategy out there. Unfortunately, it is also the most elusive and difficult to control.

This marketing method relies more on your customers than on your efforts, and can usually be traced to the quality of your product or service.

To put it another way: word of mouth marketing happens when a product or service "sells itself."

What is it?

People like to talk. Word of mouth marketing, basically, is giving them something to talk about: your business. It is building a "buzz" about your product or service, and letting your customers do the marketing legwork for you by telling friends, family, and sometimes even complete strangers if they're excited enough.

Word of mouth marketing is powerful, because it is genuine. You can't fake this phenomenon. When people believe what you have is worth mentioning to others, they're going to be enthusiastic -- and that enthusiasm helps to generate even more business for you in the form of new customers and wider market recognition.

There are many different forms word of mouth marketing can take. Just a few of them are:

Viral marketing: Crafting and distributing a high-impact message that it easy to pass along to others—often through e-mail (viral marketing will be discussed further in Chapter 5).

Community marketing: Joining or forming a shared-interest community whose members are likely to enjoy your product or service. Note that with community marketing, it is important to place the good of the community first, and marketing efforts last. Marketing will evolve naturally through participation.

Buzz marketing: Creating an air of excitement or mystery around your business, usually through news, entertainment, or underground campaigns.

Grassroots marketing: Coordinating groups of volunteers to spread your message on a personal or local level.

Cause marketing: Dedicating part of your business to a social cause, which in turn earns respect and support from others dedicated to the same cause.

Conversion creation: Catch phrases, promotions, launch parties, and other memorable tools or events designed to spread through word of mouth.

Product seeding: Identifying influential or key individuals and getting your product or information into the right hands at the right time.

How do you do it?

As previously stated, even though word of mouth is effective, it's hard to pull off. If you try to fake a buzz for your business, consumers will smell a scam and your efforts will backfire.

There are, however, a few things you can do to help encourage word of mouth advertising to start on its own.

1.   Have a quality product or service. This may sound too obvious to consider, but it is perhaps the most important factor in word of mouth marketing. Make sure your customers are getting what they pay for. Research the competition -- you're going to want to know if several other businesses are offering comparable products or services at far lower (or higher) prices than you. If possible, back your product or service with a guarantee or warrantee.

2. Put your customers first. A happy customer is one who feels their purchases are important to your business. Happy customers are potential word of mouth marketing sources. Make delivering on your promises a top priority. If you offer fast shipping, be certain your products are always delivered in a reliable and timely manner. If your service promises quick turnaround, make sure you never miss a deadline. Address customer complaints and problems immediately and personally, and consider offering refunds or bonuses for dissatisfied customers.

3. Identify and speak to your target market. Who is interested in your products or services? Where do they tend to gather -- either on or off-line? Blanket advertising is ineffective at best. Your marketing efforts should be concentrated on those venues or locations where your target consumer group is most likely to see your message. Once you create a community buzz among people whose shared interests lead them to your business, your marketing campaign becomes self-supporting.

4. Make it easy for your customers to tell others about your business. Word of mouth marketing is based on spreading your message. However, if interested customers don't have a way to share their enthusiasm with others right away, they may not remember what excited them about your product or service. Provide your face-to-face customers with business cards, flyers, or an accessible sign-up list for your company newsletter (you do have a newsletter, don't you?). Online, tools such as forums and refer-a-friend programs will help to facilitate spreading the word.

5. Listen and respond. If you receive a single complaint, you can often deal with it on a personal, individual basis. However, if you receive several similar complaints, you may need to do more than simply reply to the dissatisfied customers. Be prepared to make changes in your business according to the wants and needs of your customers. This applies to positive suggestions as well as complaints. Also, if you discover that your business is being slammed, don't be afraid to defend yourself in a logical, reasonable

manner (avoid flame wars). Customers respect businesses that are willing to admit their mistakes and will try to repair the damage.

Summary

Word of mouth marketing happens when a product or service "sells itself" through the enthusiasm of the consumer

Word of mouth marketing cannot be faked; it stems from genuine compassion on the part of both business and customer

There are many different forms word of mouth marketing can take

Word of mouth marketing cannot be engineered, but it can be encouraged The customer is the most important factor in word of mouth marketing

Word of mouth marketing is one of the least expensive and most powerful forms of Creative marketing

Canvassing

You may have seen this term used in conjunction with political campaigns, and in fact that's one of the most common reasons to employ canvassing. However, this technique can also be used effectively for Creative marketing.

What is it?

Canvassing refers to advertising that reaches out to a group of target consumers, usually in the same geographic location, on an individual level.

A simple example of a canvassing campaign would be a new pizza place sending its employees out with stacks of flyers, to be left on or under as many doors in their delivery area as possible.

Other canvassing techniques include:

Door to door introductions (think Jehovah's Witness here). Parking lot flyer distribution.

Sidewalk or mall sampling. Telephone campaigns.

How do you do it?

Though there is some monetary expense involved in most canvassing campaigns (usually to print the materials you plan to distribute), this type of marketing can be both inexpensive and effective. There are three stages to a successful canvassing campaign: planning, preparation, and distribution.

Planning: This, of course, is the most important. You have to plan the materials themselves, and you also have to determine the distribution area or method that will be most effective for you and your business.

For a local business, you will of course be interested in canvassing locally. You can distribute flyers door to door (be sure to check your area laws before you start passing out material this way), hang them on community bulletin boards or telephone poles (again, check with local ordinances here), or plan an area mailing campaign.

You can also make arrangements with other local businesses to hand out your materials (flyers, business cards, brochures, and bookmarks, to name a few) in exchange for advertising for them. If you have materials available, be sure to stay alert in regards to community events that may attract your target market.

If your business is primarily online, your canvassing area will consist of websites and forums your target customers frequent, as well as individual e-mails. Be sure to do your research and have a list of these places, along with the methods you can use to attract interest there (banner ads, forum memberships, guest blogging, articles, newsletters, and the like).

When planning your materials, make sure you spend some time getting them as attractive and interesting as possible. Comb your wording for spelling and grammatical errors -- not only can these make for a bad first impression to customers, but they can also end up with some unintended consequences. As an extreme example, imagine what would happen if the Motel Six chain missed a typo, and launched an advertising campaign for Motel Sex!

Your mistakes may not be as outrageous, but if you make a mistake in your advertising materials, your customers will be more likely to remember you for your mistakes than the quality of your products or services.

Also, make sure your material is exciting and compelling. Remember your USP? Take the aspect of your business that sets it apart from your competitors and emphasize it in your marketing copy.

If you can come up with a catchy phrase or slogan, a recognizable

icon, or a fun play on words that describes your business, this short and sweet message can go a long way on your materials.

Preparation: Once you've decided on your materials, you have to create them. If you are sending out a small batch of flyers, business cards, or brochures, you may be able to make them yourself with a high-quality printer. A commercial printer is usually more economical for larger quantities.

Places like Staples and Kinko's have become more affordable than ever, and there are several competitive online companies like VistaPrint.com to choose from as well.

You will need to supply the printer with a file to print from. With the proliferation of desktop publishing software, you will likely be able to design the materials yourself. However, be sure to invest a lot of time and make it a professional presentation. If you don't feel confident in creating great-looking and sounding promotional material, you may want to consider hiring a freelance designer or copywriter -- you'll pay a one-time price for material you can use over and over.

Distribution: This refers to actually getting the material to your customers. You can distribute flyers yourself, or enlist volunteers to help. Volunteers, partners, or anyone who's willing to spend some time helping you promote may be willing to stand in high-traffic areas like malls or transportation terminals and hand out your material.

You may be mailing out your materials, in which case your distribution involves a trip to the post office. If you're partnering with another local business, you'll simply have to drop off a stack of materials with them.

If you plan an online canvassing campaign, it's a good idea to try and coordinate the various venues and have them hit within the same time frame. Multiple banners, ads, articles, forum posts, blog entries, and e-mails that reach your target audience more than once will help to reinforce your business in their minds, and help them remember you the next time they need your product or service.

Summary

Canvassing is any marketing method that reaches multiple consumers on an individual basis

There are many forms of canvassing, including flyer and brochure distribution, sampling, telephone or door-to-door marketing, and online campaigns

Canvassing is most effective when you have researched your target market demographic and can access a number of them in the same area

Other businesses make excellent canvassing partners, since you can reach all of their customers without much effort

Canvassing relies on a strong message and well-written material to achieve results Distribution, the final step of canvassing, can take place in person, online, or through a third party

The Sign Says

Signs are everywhere. A good sign can be a great tool for your business, and in true Creative marketing style, it doesn't have to cost much.

What is it?

A sign is any at-a-glance advertisement for your business. They range in size from matchbook covers to billboards, and can be found in a wide variety of locations. Signs are familiar to just about everyone, because there are so many of them. Unfortunately, this means people often overlook them.

How do you do it?

If you want to use signs as part of your Creative marketing campaign, there are two important factors you need to consider: design and placement

What it should look like

Creating an effective sign means making it stand out from its surroundings, and giving it some individual and memorable characteristics. At the same time, you have to strike a balance between information and clutter.

You may want to consider hiring a professional designer. As with printed advertising materials, the one-time investment often proves worthwhile, since you can use the design over and over again.

However, if you feel confident that you can create your own signs, here are some tips for effective design:

Make sure it's legible from the distance most people will view it. At the least, you will include your website and/or phone number, but if no one can read your sign, they won't contact you for more information.

Speaking of information, don't include too much. The object of a sign is to get people interested in learning more about your business, so don't attempt to close a sale with just your sign.

Apply the KISS principle: Keep It Short & Simple. Elaborate designs and excessive wording will distract rather than attract attention. Ideally, your sign should contain 3 to 10 words in addition to your contact information.

Include a "grabber" element -- either a strong word or phrase in large text, or an intriguing image or company logo.

Pay attention to color scheme, and make sure they are contrasting enough to stand out so everything is easily legible. Some excellent color combinations include black on white, black on yellow, white on black, yellow on black, and blue on white.

What is not there is just as important as what is. You should incorporate approximately 30 to 40 percent of "white space" (not necessarily white, but space with no words or images on it) in the overall design of your sign.

Where to put it

After you design your sign, you'll need to figure out where to put it. Of course, there are the traditional places -- billboards, storefronts, bulletin boards, and the like. You can also get creative and find other places or venues for your signs.

Restroom signs are becoming more popular. Some businesses will allow you to advertise in their bathrooms, and one creative company has actually placed advertisements inside men's urinals with some success.

Roadside placement: Got a house on a road with decent foot or vehicle traffic? How about friends in prime locations? Try placing a sign in your front yard, and recruiting friends to do the same.

Check with community event coordinators -- you may be able to place signs at bake sales, fundraisers, and other local happenings.

Consider swapping signage space with other businesses in your area for greater exposure.

Summary

Though signs are associated with traditional advertising, they can be part of a successful Creative marketing campaign

A sign is any at-a-glance advertisement for your business

Design and placement are the two key elements for successful signs

Creative sign placement can boost your signs' effectiveness

Vehicle and Body Advertising

This space for rent: Attractive signs for your business are great, but they are stationary

--   the only people who see them are those who walk or drive by them. In many ways, mobile signs can attract more attention.

What better way to get your signs in motion than to put them on a moving vehicle... or a moving person?

What is it?

Vehicle advertising: The most obvious examples are the small signs you may have seen on city buses. Transportation companies often rent space on their fleet vehicles to advertisers as an additional source of income. This means anywhere the bus goes, your advertising will be seen by the people in the area, both foot traffic and vehicle traffic.

Other forms of vehicle advertising include:

Interior bus signs

Taxi and limo billboards Bumper stickers

Vehicle wraps Self-service

Body advertising: How about a walking, talking advertisement for your business? You can find people who are willing, for a small fee, to wear temporary tattoos advertising your product or service. These tattoos often make a great conversation piece, and can make a lot of people aware of your business.

How do you do it?

Vehicle advertising: For bus, taxi, and limo advertising, contact your local transportation companies and ask about their ad rates for fleet vehicles. You will probably need to supply your own designs for the ads, but the rates are often fairly inexpensive for the amount of exposure you'll receive. Be sure to spend a lot of time coming up with a catchy advertisement!

You can have custom bumper stickers printed for your business. It's a good idea to feature your (easy to remember) website prominently on a custom bumper sticker. Give them away to family, friends, customers, and at community events. Consider supplying free bumper stickers to other local businesses, to give away to their customers.

Vehicle wraps are partial or full vehicle advertisements that generate some interesting reactions. You pay people -- usually those who drive back and forth to work every day -- to have their personal vehicles "wrapped" with advertisements for your business.

You can also wrap your own personal vehicle, or get body or window detailing done with your business information. No matter where you drive, you will constantly be advertising your product or service!

Body advertising: Your first step here is to design a compelling temporary tattoo that people can identify quickly with your business. Again, it is a good idea to prominently feature your URL in the design, to allow prospective customers to find more information quickly.

When choosing people to wear your temporary tattoos:

Decide how much you're willing to pay each person you recruit. You may want to base this on the number of days the tattoo should remain visible and in good condition.

Specify where the tattoo should be worn. The back of the hand is a good, prominent place, though some advertisers have requested that people place them on their foreheads.

Instruct the recruits as to what information you'd like them to give when people ask about their tattoos. You may want to consider providing them with business cards, brochures, bookmarks, or other promotional items to hand out to those who show interest.

Ask them to keep track of how many people they talk to concerning the tattoos, so you can use the information in your marketing calculations.

Summary

Vehicle and body advertising serve as mobile signs for your business

There are many different forms of vehicle advertising, some more expensive than others

Body advertising is enlisting other people to place advertisements for your business on a visible part of their bodies

Vehicle and body advertisements must be eye-catching and compelling in order to attract interest

You will need an easy-to-remember URL to incorporate prominently in your vehicle or body advertising design

Don't forget to enlist yourself, your personal vehicle, and your own body as advertising tools for your business!

Promotional Items

Everyone loves getting free stuff. Promotional items combine this basic element of human psychology with marketing flair for an effective and memorable component of a Creative advertising campaign.

What is it?

A "promotional item" can be any of hundreds of different things. Basically, it's any physical item that bears a printed mention of your business. Your promotional items can be traditional or unique.

You can give them away free, award them to customers for buying certain things or participating in special offers, and even sell them (if they are high quality and in demand) as an additional source of income.

Following is a list of a few traditional and not-so-traditional promotional items that can be customized for your business:

Brochures and sales catalogues Bookmarks

Printed newsletters Glossy flyers

Business cards Magnets

Bumper stickers Key chains

Coffee mugs Shot glasses Water goblets Tee shirts
Sweatshirts

Baseball caps Sweatbands Bandannas

Stress balls

Stuffed animals Coasters

Posters

Matchbooks Lanyards

Napkins

Toothpick holders Pens/pencils

Calendars Tote bags

Travel clocks Travel mirrors Combs/brushes Box cutters
Towels/washcloths

How do you do it?

Effective promotional products are intriguing, fitting, and carry just enough information without overburdening your customers. Here are some tips on creating effective promotional items:

Design with signs in mind. Keep the information on promotional products simple and to the point -- include your business name, slogan, and contact information (phone number and/or website). After all, if the item is slathered with text, no one is going to want to actually use it.

Choose items that reflect your business. If you run a catering company, custom napkins and other kitchen items are good choices; whereas combs, brushes, and towels might not be such a good fit. However, just about any promotional item can be adapted to any business with a little creativity.

Make your items fun and attractive. Bookmarks are great, but how many people do you know that actually use them? Unless your main product is a printed book, if you have a bunch of bookmarks made they will probably end up in the trash. Consider what your customers like to do, and base your promotional item decision on your best guess at what will interest them. Custom puzzles, anyone?

Shop around for the best deals. Unless you're creating your promotional items yourself (and it is certainly possible, though time-consuming), you will likely look for a custom printer or manufacturer to emblazon your message on hundreds of items. There are dozens of great places online, including Café Press (www.cafepress.com), which lets you create and purchase your own items at cost, with bulk discounts for larger orders. You might also want to purchase bulk novelty items from a company like the Oriental Trading Company (www.orientaltrading.com) and modify the items yourself.

Distribute your items freely and often. Always keep several promotional items with you, and hand them out constantly. You never know when you'll meet someone who will later become your customer -- and you will at the very least make a bunch of folks happy by giving them free stuff! Don't forget the power of giveaways in conjunction with your main business. Offer to give your promotional items to customers with every purchase. Post the freebie notice in your physical location or on your website, as well as message boards and freebie forums for more exposure.

Summary

A promotional item is any physical, tangible item that bears a message or advertisement for your business

There are hundreds of promotional items to choose from You can make just about anything into a promotional item
Promotional items should relate to your business in some way

Effective promotional items bear simple messages and contact information The best promotional items are fun or useful for your customers
You should always keep a supply of promotional items on hand

Chapter 4 – Digital Creative Marketing

Whether your business is a traditional store, a work-from-home operation, or a completely online venture, a strong web presence is a must in today's fast-paced marketing world. In the age of instant information, businesses without websites have a decided disadvantage.

One of the most important things to keep in mind when it comes to online marketing is that despite the instantaneous nature of the Internet, there are no overnight success methods. Just like a live marketing campaign, your online Creative marketing efforts will require time and effort in order to succeed.

In this chapter, we'll discuss the ins and outs of online promotion, and learn some Creative marketing techniques you can use to further your business on the Internet, whether or not it's based online.

Establishing yourself

If you want customers, you need to make people aware of your website. You also have to make sure your website is a good place to be. Your basic goals with online marketing are to generate traffic to your website, and to keep visitors there when they arrive (and keep them coming back).

We'll talk about this in reverse order, since you need your website up and running before you start attracting visitors.

Website basics

A website can be a very powerful marketing tool. However, a bad website can have a powerful but opposing effect: driving off not only current visitors, but also everyone they know, when they start telling everyone on the 'net how terrible your website looks, or how difficult it is to navigate.

Keep in mind that there are millions of websites out there, and if yours does not attract a visitor's attention with their first look, they'll simply go to the next page of search results and give their business to someone else.

Does your website pass the first-look test? Here are some rules to keep in mind:

Your URL, or website address (www.YourWebSite.com) should be easy to remember and spell, and contain very few, if any, special characters or alternate spellings. This not only looks more professional when visitors find a link to your website online, but it also makes it much easier to translate real-world advertisements into website visitors. You should include your URL on all of your physical marketing material.

Your home page should be visually pleasing, easy to read, and not cluttered with text. Make sure all of your important information is contained in the top portion of your home page (the area visible on a screen when a visitor first arrives at the site) -- but do not try to cram everything on the home page. Include links to essential pages rather than lengthy descriptions of everything.

Flash animation is great, but a huge flash presentation on your home page not only slows down your load time (to the point where visitors will not bother waiting for the page to display), but also turns off many casual Internet users. If you must use Flash animation, keep it to a minimum and don't use it to convey essential information.

If you have a newsletter, include an e-mail link or a subscription box on every page of your website. The more visible your options are, the greater the chances people will find them.

Your website should be an informative place. A hard-sell website ("This product/service is amazing! Buy it now!") does not appeal to most Web browsers. Be

sure to post news and current events concerning your business, and consider providing informative articles that educate visitors on topics pertaining to your products or services.

Update often. Keeping your content fresh not only makes search engines happy, it also provides visitors with a reason to keep coming back!

Make your content keyword-rich without being blatant. Brainstorm a list of search terms Internet users might type into a search engine when looking for a website like yours, and use each of those terms a few times. Do not clump together lists of keywords; instead, sprinkle them throughout your content. The practice of keyword stuffing can get your website banned from search engines.

Be user-friendly! Test your website using several different screen resolutions to make sure the text and images are not too crowded or spread out. Check your links and navigation controls frequently -- few things are more frustrating to an Internet user than dead or outdated links. Make sure every page includes a link to your home page and a link to your sales or "landing" page, at the very least.

Internet marketing basics

Just about all "traditional" forms of Internet marketing can be classified as Creative marketing. This is because Internet advertising is generally inexpensive or free, involves an investment of your time and effort, and must be presented in a unique manner if you want to stand out from the millions of other websites competing for attention.

It is a good idea to incorporate basic Internet marketing into your Creative campaign. If you have never promoted a website before, you may not be familiar with the basic concepts of spreading the e-word.

Here are a few ideas to get you started (remember, all these tactics should be implemented after your website is optimized, fine-tuned, double-checked and ready for business):

The more search engines your website is listed on, the greater the chance customers will stumble across it. The "big" search engines such as Google and

Yahoo! do not allow manual submissions, but your website will automatically be picked up within a few weeks by their web trawlers. However, smaller search engines like AltaVista, Dogpile, and ExactSeek may not automatically include your site. There are many free search engine submission programs online that will submit your website to multiple engines for inclusion. Be sure to have a list of keywords and a brief (two to three sentences) description of your website available while you're submitting.

If you have a newsletter, you can list your website in multiple newsletter or e-zine directories in the same way you submit to search engine. Having a free, regular newsletter or e-zine that contains interesting and informative material is a great way to build customer loyalty and attract new business online. Your subscribers will be more likely to purchase your products or services, since they will see your business multiple times.

Banner ad exchange programs are another possibility for Internet exposure. When you design your banner ad, keep in mind the rules for creating an effective sign and apply them to the banner. If you don't have any computer experience, there are several programs that will allow you to generate a banner ad using their template for free. Then, seek similar or complementary websites to your business and offer to host their banner in exchange for hosting theirs on your website.

Pay-per-click (PPC) advertising is effective in many cases, and though it does require a monetary investment, the amount is small (usually 2 to 5 cents per visitor). One example of a good pay-per-click program is Google AdWords (http://adwords.google.com) -- the program does not require minimum monthly spending, and the average bidding rate for lesser search terms is 2 to 3 cents. Google also includes a keyword generator to help you write more effective ads. More information is available through the preceding link.

Going Viral

Viral marketing is one of the most powerful forms of Internet advertising available. It takes basic online marketing a step further: basically, you get the ball rolling, and hundreds of other Internet users pick it up and run with it.

What is it?

Viral marketing is more or less the Internet term for word-of-mouth. The term "viral marketing" refers to any advertising method that encourages people who receive a message to pass it on to others.

One classic example of a viral marketing strategy was demonstrated by Microsoft Networks Hotmail program. Hotmail was one of the first free web-based e-mail providers.

In order to let people know about the program, Microsoft included a tag or signature at the bottom of every outgoing e-mail their customers sent, reading: "Get your private, free e-mail at http://www.hotmail.com", that was linked to Hotmail's main page. People receiving messages from users with Hotmail accounts set up their own, and then e-mailed more people with the same tag on every message. The number of Hotmail users ballooned in no time.

In essence, Microsoft invented the e-mail signature, another powerful marketing tool now used by millions online.

Keep in mind that viral marketing does not simply spread your message from person to person. Effective viral marketing spreads from person to people, making your advertising program an exponential success.

How do you do it?

The best way to engage in viral marketing online is to make it easy for your customers to spread your message. There are quite a few ways to do this:

Newsletters or e-zines: Since most newsletters and e-zines are delivered via e-mail, it's easy for your customers to hit forward and pass them on to several friends.

However, this will only happen if you include good, quality information in your electronic publication. Rather than simply advertising your products or services, consider writing articles, hosting guest columns, and generally providing your customers with something fun.

Article syndication: Once you have written articles for your newsletter or e-zine, share the knowledge by uploading them to article syndication websites.
These are
"article banks" used by web masters looking for fresh content for their own websites.

Essentially, you are giving anyone permission to reprint your article, with the caveat that your authorship and a link to your website is included. Article syndication creates inbound links that boost your website's search engine rank, and make it more likely customers will find you.

Refer-a-friend programs: Got something valuable to give your customers, such as bonus products or promotional items? Consider using a refer-a-friend program: in exchange for providing you with a number of e-mail addresses to which you can send a one-time announcement about your business, you can give your customers something they'll enjoy, and make them eager to tell their friends about your website.

Link-swapping and banner placement: As mentioned in the previous section, the more links there are on the Internet leading to your website, the greater your exposure will be. Offer to host other websites' links and banner ads on your site in exchange for a reciprocal link from theirs. Also, keep in mind that inbound links (links that point to your website, and are not linked back from your website) carry more weight with search engines than outbound or reciprocal links. Try to post as many inbound links as you can.

Giveaways, contests, and freebies: Once again, everyone loves to get something for nothing. Sponsoring contests and giveaways will naturally generate the urge for your customers to tell others about your website, so everyone they know can get the free deal or enter the contest. Don't hesitate to give away the occasional product or service in exchange for the marketing value it can bring your business!

Online communities and forums: Joining forums and communities dedicated to topics that will interest your customers is a great way to get your name out there.
Remember, online etiquette dictates that you do not simply join a forum and immediately post advertisements. Spend some time getting to know other forum members, and they will be happy to tell others in the community about you and your business.

As with other forms of advertising, your message has to be compelling and interesting, or no one will want to pass it on. Make sure to spend as much time developing your advertising message as you do spreading it around. Don't forget to include your USP, any promotions or freebies you may be running, and your website and contact information.

Summary

Viral marketing is the Internet form of word-of-mouth

The keys to viral marketing are to create a compelling message and make it easy for people to pass it on

Viral marketing represents an exponential increase in online exposure for your business

There are several different viral marketing methods you can take advantage of for your website

Viral marketing messages must be interesting, informative, or valuable in order to be successfully spread

Beating the Blog Drum

Do you blog? Even if you don't, chances are you have already seen several blogs online, though you might not be aware of this relatively new website format.
Blogs

create a sense of community and provide an outlet for many different types of information, both business and personal.

What is it?

Blog, short for web log, is a specialized type of website that acts like an electronic journal. Blog users can type in text, upload pictures and sound, and instantly post it to the site. Blog software formats each entry in the blog style you select, automatically creates entry archives and permanent links to each page, and allows for easy customization.

Most blogs also allow comments from visitors. There are comment screening options you can use to disallow anonymous comments, comments from non-bloggers, or comments altogether. However, the comments feature is one of the most powerful components of a blog, because visitors can enjoy instant interaction with you.

Blogs allow you to speak with your customers on a personal level. Once Internet users get to know the person behind the business, they will be more likely to purchase your products or services. Trust is a valuable commodity online, and blogs help you build up a trust bank.

Best of all, most blogs are free to create and use, so you won't have to spend a penny on your blog.

A few of the most popular blog providers are:

Blogger -- www.blogger.com: Owned by Google. Fully featured free blogs with customizable templates, easy to use

LiveJournal - www.livejournal.com: Similar to Blogger, offers paid upgrades for additional special features

WordPress - www.wordpress.com: Another popular free blogger platform with millions of users, easy interfaces and lots of template choices

Blogs have become so popular, there are millions of bloggers (people with blogs) online communicating tons of information, opinions, and chats every day. In fact, the blog collective on the Internet has become powerful enough to merit its own term: the blogosphere. The blogosphere as a whole is extremely influential, and often when one blog carries an item of interest, others will pick it up and spread it across the Internet.

How do you do it?

Using a blog for business purposes is a twofold process. First, you have to build a readership for your blog. Then, you can enlist other bloggers to help you get more exposure for yours.

Building a readership

Like your website, you should plan to keep your blog informative and entertaining, and update regularly. Many bloggers post to their blogs daily, and often include links to other websites with news or information they believe may interest their readers. It is a good idea to choose a posting schedule (daily, Monday through Friday, bi-weekly, weekly -- whatever you're comfortable keeping up with) and stick to it.

The single most effective way to gain readers for your blog is to visit other people's blogs and leave thoughtful comments on their posts. Do not simply comment that you have a blog and you want them to visit; this is viewed as spam, or at the very least, rude.

Of course, contacting individual bloggers is a time-consuming process. Another way to attract readers is to list your blog in as many blog directories as you can find. This way, Internet users will be able to find your blog through search engines.

Post a link to your blog on your website, and include one in your e-mail signature. The more people know about your blog, the more likely you will be to get visitors.

Working in the blogosphere

Other bloggers are an excellent marketing resource. Most blogging software includes an easy tool to add links to your sidebar. You can link to several other blogs that may be of interest to your readers -- and in most cases, the bloggers you link to will automatically link back to your blog, since this is considered common courtesy. Some bloggers will list an e-mail address you can contact them through to exchange blog links. Take advantage of these when you find them. You can also participate in guest blogging -- writing an entry for someone else's blog for a day. Since bloggers always need fresh content, many are happy to host other people's articles as long as they pertain to their readers. Find blogs that are similar to yours and request to be a guest blogger. Remember to include a link to your website at the end of your post!

Summary

Blogs are a specialized form of website that act like online journals

The millions of blogs online are collectively known as the blogosphere Bloggers (people who blog) and blog readers are very influential online

Most blogs are free to set up, and have easy templates that don't require HTML coding knowledge

Like your website, your blog should be informative, entertaining, and updated regularly Visit other people's blogs and link to them to get increased traffic for your blog

Becoming a guest blogger is a great way to get more exposure for your business.

Chapter 5 – Rules and Regulations

Following the rules is an important step in Creative marketing. Some people view Creative marketing tactics as too aggressive, and many a marketer has been threatened with legal action.

However, if you're familiar with what you can and cannot do, you will not have to worry about this. Make sure you protect yourself!

Fairness in Advertising

Honesty is still the best policy. Consumers don't appreciate being lied to, and nothing spreads faster -- both online and in your community -- than news of a dishonest business.

Therefore, it's important that you practice fairness in advertising.

What It Means

Fairness in advertising is really a simple concept: don't claim your product or service does something that it doesn't. For example, a diet pill company claiming their product will "make you lose 50 pounds overnight!" is clearly mistaken -- this is a physical impossibility, unless you amputate your legs. Even with a quantifier like "practically" or "almost" (You'll lose 50 pounds practically overnight!), the statement remains implausible. Every person's idea of "practically" is different.

What would be fair for our fictitious diet pill company to claim? It depends on what the product actually does. In this scenario, the company may be able to state that their diet pill helps you lose weight "faster than the leading brands" or even that you may notice results "practically overnight" (not 50 pounds worth of results, of course!).

Your wording is essential when practicing fairness in advertising. You can get creative, but there is a fine line between creativity and false claims. In most cases, it's best to let your product or service speak for itself.

Customer testimonials are an excellent way to incorporate fairness in advertising. Getting real statements from the people who have used your product or service not only keeps you honest, but also allows consumers to trust you more, because the opinions are coming from someone who has no vested interest in your business.

Don't lie to your customers, and they will thank you with their business.

Spam Isn't Healthy

One of the most pervasive myths in online advertising today is this: the more people you e-mail, the more money you'll make. But if you're using bulk e-mail to get there, you're on the wrong track.

No one likes spam. In the Internet world, the term "spam" refers to any e-mail advertising a product or service that you did not ask to receive (and not the lunchmeat-in-a-can pictured above). There are a lot of marketing "gurus" who insist that sending cold bulk e-mails still gets results -- and that may have been true when the Internet was still in its infancy, but today's online community is more perceptive than ever, and it's almost impossible to slip by the collective spam radar.

If you look, you can find several hundred places that will sell you lists of thousands of e-mail addresses for a few dollars. The temptation to buy these lists is strong... who can resist thousands of potential customers in one shot, without the many hours of research it takes to build a solid opt-in list of your own?

You can! Here's why you should:

Spamming alienates potential customers. When people receive spam, often their first reaction is to delete it unread, and most will block all further communication from that particular e-mail address: yours.

Many Internet users hate spam so much, they will take action to shut you down. This can range from reporting you to your ISP (Internet service provider), to flaming (sending hate mail) or "mail bombs" (sending hundreds or thousands of files with very large attachments designed to crash your server).

Your business can be blacklisted. There is an actual Internet advertiser's blacklist that warns consumers about spammers, and you don't want to be connected with that list.

Spamming just plain doesn't work! There are so many dangerous scams online today that most Internet users are reluctant to even open any unsolicited messages. Even if you write the most brilliant and enticing advertising message in the world, if you send it through bulk e-mail, no one will ever read it.

In short: don't spam. Do the work and create your own list of people who actually want to hear what you have to say. Your business will benefit enormously, and you won't be branded as a charlatan.

Weird Laws and Ordinances

As a Creative marketer, it's important for you to obey the law. If a customer feels you are trying to con them, skirt legal issues, or harass them into buying your product or service, you could end up with a lot more trouble than a lost sale.

You can familiarize yourself with basic marketing dos and don'ts through the Federal Trade Commission (FTC), the government organization that regulates and protects

consumers in the United States. Browse their website at www.ftc.gov for more information on advertising guidance, antitrust laws, and FTC procedures regarding consumer complaints.

You should also check with your local Chamber of Commerce, and request information on advertising laws that affect your business. Find the nearest Chamber to you here: http://www.uschamber.com/chambers/directory/default

Does your city or state have strange laws that forbid a certain Creative marketing method? The website Dumb Laws (www.dumblaws.com) provides a collection of weird, outrageous and outlandish laws that are still on the books. Here is a sampling of some laws that might hinder your marketing efforts:

In Alabama, it is illegal to impersonate a person of the clergy -- so don't dress up as a priest to promote your business.

You can be fined $25 for flirting in New York. Beware of approaching strangers!

Speaking of truth in advertising, a jail term of up to one year awaits you in Louisiana for making a false promise.

Watch out, mobile billboard advertisers in Ohio: the Ohio driver's education manual states that you must honk the horn when you pass another vehicle.

In Texas, it is illegal to sell one's eye. Keep your body parts close at hand.

Florida forbids "unnatural acts" with another person... so forget playing Twister on the sidewalk. Also, it's illegal to skateboard without a license.

Unless you own at least two cows, you may not wear cowboy boots in California.

Seasonal business owners should note that in Maine, you will be fined for displaying Christmas decorations after January 14.

Your profits will come in handy in Illinois, where you can be arrested for vagrancy if you don't have at least one dollar on your person.

What strange laws does your state have? Perhaps one of them will give you an idea for your Creative marketing campaign!

Chapter 6 – Welcome to the Jungle

Are you ready to become a Creative?

Without a doubt, Creative marketing is an extremely effective strategy for any small business. Since you typically will not have a huge advertising budget, it makes more sense to invest effort and time, and reap the rewards of your careful planning and creativity.

Some points to remember:

You will get out of your Creative marketing campaign what you put into it. If you do not invest the effort, you will not reap the rewards.

A successful Creative marketing campaign is ongoing, and consists of more than one strategy or tactic.

Be patient: Creative success will not come to you overnight, but it will come!

Think outside the box (in fact, try to come up with your own term for thinking outside the box as an exercise in creativity). The unique aspects of your business will generate better profits when you leverage them.

Do not view other businesses as your competition. Instead, view them as potential partners and cultivate mutually beneficial relationships.

Never pass up an opportunity to market (but keep it casual where it's appropriate to refrain from being pushy).

Be prepared to watch your business leap forward!

Creative marketing is not just a strategy... it's a state of mind. When you learn to think like a Creative, you will greatly improve your business marketing skills -- not to mention your profits.

A List Of 100 Niche Marketing And Selling Concepts !

This Book Contains Ideas For Some Larger Popular Niches

And Smaller Profitable Targeted Niches.

(First Free Manuscript As Bonus!)

By : "Santiago Johnson Smith"

This publication is designed to provide accurate and authoritative information with regard to the subject matter covered.

It is sold with the understanding that the author and the publisher are not engaged in rendering legal, intellectual property, accounting or other professional advice.

If legal advice or other professional assistance is required, the services of a competent professional should be sought.

The author and and distributor individually or corporately, do not accept any responsibility for any liabilities resulting from the actions of any parties involved.

Some businesses soar towards success, while others falter. Why is this? What do these businesses encompass that others do not?

They have two vital things that failing businesses do not have. An understanding of human psychology that's backed with a niche idea they believe in.

People make decisions based on their emotions. We all desire to look and feel good. We all want to have a sense of security and community. You and I, him and her, we're all seeking those life-changing adventures that make us come alive.

Businesses that understand the human psyche create a special connection with their niche market. While others in that niche fall short and feel impersonal.

Human psychology ties into your copywriting, content marketing, niche market selection, and product creation. When you apply humanness to these areas in your business, success will follow.

Here's How to Handle Niche Marketing. Plus, 3 Examples to Get You Started.

If you're in an industry that feels oversaturated with other businesses and competitors, standing out can sometimes seem impossible. But differentiating your brand in a crowded market is achievable with niche marketing.

What Is Niche Marketing?

Niche marketing is an advertising strategy that focuses on a unique target market. Instead of marketing to everyone who could benefit from a product or service, this strategy focuses exclusively on one group—a niche market—or demographic of potential customers who would most benefit from the offerings.

A niche market could stand apart from others because of:

Geographic area

Lifestyle

Occasion

Profession

Style

Culture

Activity or habits

Behavior

Demographic

Need

Feature reduction or addition

The benefit of niche marketing is that it allows brands to differentiate themselves, appear as a unique authority, and resonate more deeply with a distinct set of customers. Rather than blend in with the many other brands that offer the same type of product or service, a brand can use niche marketing to stand out, appear more valuable, reach its growth potential, and build a stronger, longer-lasting connection with its ideal audience.

3 Niche Marketing Examples

Niche markets are often segments of larger industries and verticals. Here are a few brands that found a way to drill down into their industry to market to a niche audience.

Divvies Vegan and Nut Free

There are hundreds of brands that sell sweet treats and snack foods such as cookies, brownies, popcorn, and cupcakes. While most people can choose from dozens of brands to find options that satisfy their cravings, there is a group of people who cannot. Those people have allergies or food restrictions that relate to animal products and nuts.

Divvies saw this underserved segment in the sweets industry and created a brand that exclusively targeted this group. Selling cookies and cupcakes is not a unique idea, but selling them as vegan and nut-free options differentiated Divvies in an already saturated market, allowing them to stand out and build a loyal customer base.

Lefty's: The Left Hand Store

Identifying an underserved community in a large market is a smart way to approach niche marketing. Like Divvies, Lefty's: The Left Hand Store found a widely underserved community of people – those who favor their left hand instead of their right hand.

Because 90% of the population uses its right hand, left-handers have widely had to adjust to using products designed for "righties." Lefty's saw this as an opportunity. They created a store that sells products designed exclusively for the other 10% and found success reaching this smaller, often ignored audience.

UNTUCKit

The commercial clothing industry is a vertical that can feel like everything has been done. But UNTUCKit proves there are still creative ways to create a new space in a long-established market segment. By making even just a small change, you can build a whole new sector in a traditional space.

UNTUCKit probably wasn't looking to create a new type of shirt. They were more likely focused on serving a specific community of people: those who didn't like to tuck in their shirts. To give those people want they wanted, UNTUCKit created a new line of products that solved a problem that a lot of people were having, but didn't know how to solve.

How to Find a Niche Market

After seeing a few examples, you will be better equipped for identifying micromarketing opportunities in your own industry.

To find and flush out an idea for a niche market in your vertical, go through the following 4-step process.

1. Identify your strengths and interests.

Start by considering what you offer and what you're good at. The best niche marketing strategies play into your brand's unique strengths and perspectives. So reflect on the special and exceptional qualities of your brand, team, and offerings.

Also consider the areas that you enjoy working in and the people you like working with. Niche marketing is an opportunity to drill down and focus on the sector of people you most want to connect with, so decide who you are most eager to serve.

What specific problems do you solve?

What problems can you solve better than your competitors?

Where do you especially excel?

What do you know a lot about?

Who do you and your team like to serve?

2. Do industry research.

Once you have an idea about the type of niche marketing you want to do, validate that it is a reasonable idea. Do a competitive analysis to see if there are competitors in this space and if there are, what those brands are already doing.

Also look to see if any openings in your target market may have been missed and if there is legitimate demand in the vertical.

Use Ubersuggest to see what ideas might be out there. Ubersuggest is a keyword suggestion tool that provides variations of a phrase or word that people are searching for. Enter a broad term to engage in keyword discovery and get ideas for how to drill down into a topic.

You can also browse Amazon product categories. Because Amazon is such a massive online retailer, it's a great place to get inspiration for product categories you may not have thought of. Spend some time browsing to see how to drill down into popular product categories.

Last but not least, use Alexa's Keyword Difficulty Tool to gauge search interest. Knowing what people are searching for will offer insight into customer interest and help you see what type of competition already exists in a niche market. Use Alexa's Keyword Difficulty Tool to search for top keywords and see how often the phrases are used by searchers (popularity score) and how competitive the term is (competition score).

3. Get to know your ideal customer.

Another way to gain insight and spark inspiration for niche marketing is to look closely at your target audience and identify what they really want and need. Getting to know your ideal customer can help you offer them a better product, service, or message.

To research your ideal audience, use Alexa's Audience Overlap Tool. Enter your site or a site that has an audience you would like to reach. The tool will help you find similar websites that share the audience and explore them in an interactive visualization. From here, you can look for trends that tell you what else the audience might be interested in. You can identify ways to focus in on your ideal customer's needs and find opportunities to market what you offer.

For example, a yoga studio might enter in an online scheduling site for fitness and wellness classes and see that audiences also frequently visit others web site. If those sites are all boutique-style shops with unique clothes, decor, and gifts, the yoga studio might see this as an opportunity for creating a specialty product shop or campaign just for yoga enthusiasts.

4. Choose, test, adjust, and repeat.

Like most marketing strategies, you can't just set up a niche marketing campaign and assume it will achieve the results you want. You must test your initial idea, review the results, and continue to adjust accordingly. You may find that your first idea for niche marketing didn't work, but that a simple tweak could hit a sweet spot that draws in audiences and leads to lifelong customers. Perhaps a full boutique shop for yoga enthusiasts didn't catch attention, but you noticed more than half of the shoppers you had bought artwork. You may then want to test and see if artwork for yogis is an idea worth exploring.

1) - You could compete in the dental/vision niche. Many businesses change markets to raise their sales. A lot of micro niches are more profitable like toothbrushes.

2) - You should enter the diet/nutrition market. Almost all entrepreneurs add industries to increase their orders. Repeatedly smaller markets are extra valuable like carb-free foods.

3) - You can move in the education/college industry. Plenty of webmasters transform niches to refine their payments. Sometimes more targeted industries are less competitive like microbiology.

4) - You might battle in the science specialty. Various advertisers switch markets to regulate their wealth. Frequently tinnier niches are more beneficial like atoms.

5) - You could attempt the energy market. Tons of companies differentiate industries to reinforce their riches. Many times littler markets are easier to market like windmills.

6) - You should try the entertainment trade. Millions of business owners replace niches to better their profits. Occasionally undersized industries are more targeted like theaters.

7) - You can encounter the environment niche. Some CEOs modify markets to seize more earnings. Most times teeny niches are extra lucrative like trees.

8) - You might participate in the exotic/adult market. Lots of promoters swap industries to revise their money. Consistently miniature markets are more practical like lageria.

9) - You could take on the fashion industry. Oodles of store owners diversify niches to safeguard their assets. Various times rare industries are less challenging like shorts.

10) - You should attack the dad/mom specialty. A number of stores innovate markets to secure their cash flow. Regularly scarce niches are extra rewarding like single parents.

11) - You can challenge the fiction market. Heaps of services metamorphosis industries to refine their bank account. Several times puny markets are more successful like Sci-Fi.

12) - You might complete in the family trade. Most product venders remodel niches to strengthen their investments. Periodically mini industries are extra sweet like heritage.

13) - You could contend with the electronics/technology niche. Scores of retailers refine markets to stretch their deposits . Numerous times minute niches are more sustaining like computing.

14) - You should mirror the frugal/save money market. Certain establishments vary industries to transform their finances. Multiple times light markets are extra useful like coupons.

15) - You can pattern the gambling/lottery industry. Hordes of web sites shift niches to upgrade their funds. A lot of subtle industries are more worthwhile like scratch off tickets.

16) - You might rival the games specialty. Countless employers transition markets to win more returns . Repeatedly uncommon niches are extra gainful like poker.

17) - You could partake in the garden market. Masses of marketers trade industries to amplify their bottom line. Sometimes unique markets are more instrumental like soil.

18) - You should perform in the gifts trade. Gobs of storefronts revise niches to blow up their income streams. Frequently original industries are more cost effective like gift baskets.

19) - You can pursue the government niche. Several shops vary markets to boast their capital. Many times thinner niches are better investments like congress.

20) - You might approach the health market. Thousands of corporations exchange industries to broaden their commissions. Occasionally dainty markets are more opportunist like blood sugar.

21) - You could labor in the hobbies industry. Umpteen executives reverse niches to bulk up their transactions. Most times frail industries are extra wholesome like kiting.

22) - You should work in the holidays specialty. Piles of managers flip-flop markets to dilate their profits. Consistently untypical niches are more attractive like Christmas.

23) - You can sell in the home remedies market. Numerous proprietors substitute industries to inflate their wallet. Various times unusual markets are extra worthy like vinegar.

24) - You might market in the humor trade. Crowds of ownerships alternate niches to swell their pocket book. Regularly little know industries are more helpful like comedy videos.

25) - You could advertise in the music/instruments niche. Multiple distributors diversify markets to widen their dollars. Several times select niches are more favorable like guitars.

26) - You should promote in the politics market. An array of enterprises modify industries to spread out their currency. Periodically seldom heard markets are extra advantageous like the law.

27) - You can publicize in the radio/television industry. Groups of stores attract niches to escalate their financial numbers. Numerous times exclusive industries are extra popular like reality shows.

28) - You might tackle the relationship specialty. Surges of services flex markets to skyrocket their billfold. Multiple times prime niches are more convertible like communication.

29) - You could venture in the safety/secure market. Herds of product venders expand industries to blossom their sponsors. A lot of novel markets are extra pleasing like locks.

30) - You should target the marketing/advertising trade. Bunches of retailers fix niches to build up their treasure. Repeatedly oddball industries are more gratifying like classifieds.

31) - You can go for the seniors niche. Many establishments implant markets to sprout their balance sheet. Sometimes strange niches are more eligible like social security.

32) - You might access the sexuality market. Almost all web sites adjustment industries to erect more payments. Frequently secondary markets are extra viable like straight/gay.

33) - You could break into the shopping industry. Plenty of employers amend niches to amass their pockets. Many times sub industries are less risky like wholesale products.

34) - You should infiltrate the singles specialty. Various marketers overhaul markets to manufacture extra greenbacks. Occasionally deeper niches are really affordable like dating sites.

35) - You can invade the self help market. Tons of storefronts restore industries to springboard their credits. Most times fresh markets are more economical like hypnosis.

36) - You might jump in the social networking trade. Millions of shops remodel niches to catapult their overall purse. Consistently new industries are extra desirable like photo sharing.

37) - You could penetrate the society/culture niche. Some corporations edit markets to propel their checks. Various times the latest niches are more important like traditions.

38) - You should sign on to the software market. Lots of executives revamp industries to advance their bucks. Regularly news worthy markets are extra effective like utilities.

39) - You can emerge in the sports industry. Oodles of managers face-lift niches to proceed increase their spenders. Several times distinct industries take less effort like football.

40) - You might appear in the space specialty. A number of proprietors combine markets to accelerate their patrons. Periodically proven niches are more suitable like planets.

41) - You could exist in the tattoos market. Heaps of ownerships merger industries to pull in more dollars. Numerous times modern markets are extra tactical like black work.

42) - You should spring into the taxes trade. Most distributors connect niches to surge their paying participates. Multiple times current industries are more handy like tax write offs.

43) - You can hop on the lifestyle niche. Scores of enterprises unify markets to hike up their community. A lot of undersized niches are extra possible like vegetation.

44) - You might land in the teens market. Certain stores junction industries to fill up their piggyback. Repeatedly long keyword niches markets are more fit like parties.

45) - You could step into the insurance/legal industry. Hordes of services affiliate niches to gather more receipts. Sometimes up to date industries are extra healthy like car insurance.

46) - You should check into the video games specialty. Countless product venders consolidate markets to magnify their proceeds. Frequently brand new niches are more fertile like portable games.

47) - You can pop into the travel/vacation market. Masses of retailers partnership industries to deepen their savings. Many times descriptive markets are extra fruitful like resorts.

48) - You might turn up in the military trade. Gobs of establishments mix niches to add to their fortune. Occasionally weird industries are more thriving like weapons.

49) - You could embrace the weather niche. Several web sites formulate markets to shoot up their total yield. Most times micro niches are extra applicative like storms.

50) - You should seize the self defense/weapons market. Thousands of employers regulate industries to flood their network. Consistently smaller markets are more achievable like guns.

51) - You can welcome the animals industry. Umpteen marketers blueprint more niches to accelerate their subscribers. Various times more targeted industries are extra reachable like cat.

52) - You might encompass the automobiles specialty. Piles of storefronts start more markets to acquire their readers. Regularly tinnier niches are more attainable like trucks.

53) - You could endorse the babies market. Numerous shops tackle extra industries to add their friends. Several times littler markets are extra profitable like breast feeding.

54) - You should affiliate in the birthdays trade. Crowds of corporations stir up more niches to assemble extra followers. Periodically undersized industries are more positive like cakes.

55) - You can tap into the business niche. Multiple executives blend markets to attract extra leads. Numerous times teeny niches are extra reasonable like Internet business.

56) - You might follow the candy/chocolate market. An array of managers direct more industries to increase their prospects. Multiple times miniature markets are more suitable like candy bars.

57) - You could utilize the celebrities industry. Groups of proprietors propel more niches to bolster their opt-ins. A lot of rare industries are extra promising like singers.

58) - You should embark upon the crime nice. Surges of ownerships principle markets to boost their members. Repeatedly scarce niches are more wealthy like crime prevention.

59) - You can test the child care market. Herds of distributors revise industries to build up their visitors. Sometimes puny markets are extra rich like babysitting.

60) - You might experiment with the trade. Bunches of enterprises process more niches to create extra fans. Frequently mini industries are more abundant like safety.

61) - You could toy with the cleaning niche. Many stores scheme in extra markets to construct more traffic. Many times minute niches are extra prosperous like stain removal.

62) - You should investigate the climate market. Almost all services arrange extra industries to grow their list. Occasionally light markets are more lush like snow removal.

63) - You can tryout the community industry. Plenty of product venders configured new niches to dig up fresh customers. Most times subtle industries are extra becoming like networking.

64) - You might figure out the computer/Internet specialty. Various retailers add markets to enhance their client amount. Consistently uncommon niches are more extensive like blogging.

65) - You could profit the communications market. Tons of establishments supplant industries to enlarge their referrals. Various times unique markets are extra sustainable like cell phones.

66) - You should make money in the conspiracy theories trade. Millions of web sites coexistent niches to enrich their income. Regularly original industries are more available like UFOs.

67) - You can study the construction niche. Some employers interconnect markets to ensure plenty of buyers. Several times thin niches are extra masterful like barns.

68) - You might learn from the countries/states market. Lots of marketers glue together industries to expand their affiliates. Periodically dainty markets are more venturesome like just Texas.

69) - You could benefit from the cooking/food industry. Oodles of storefronts maneuver more niches to extend their shoppers. Numerous times frail industries are extra manageable like sandwiches.

70) - You should take advantage of the poems specialty. A number of shops plan markets to fortify their endorsers. Multiple times untypical niches are more serviceable like poem publishing.

71) - You can earn income from the crafts market. Heaps of corporations step into extra industries to fill new subscriptions. A lot of unusual markets are extra significant like beading.

72) - You might make sales from the credit card trade. Most executives chain niches together to gain more advertisers. Repeatedly little know industries are more hot like interest rates.

73) - You could prosper in the legal niche. Scores of managers reroute markets to generate extra clicks. Sometimes select niches are extra trendy like attorneys.

74) - You should be successful in the dating/singles market. Certain proprietors tie together industries to grab more spenders. Frequently seldom heard markets are more sound like first dates.

75) - You can find abundance in the decorating industry. Hordes of ownerships alternate niches to develop extra paying admirers. Many times exclusive industries are extra safe like painting.

76) - You might have prosperity in the invention specialty. Countless distributors suggest extra markets to skyrocket more resellers. Occasionally prime niches are more secure like creativity.

77) - You could thrive in the investing market. Masses of enterprises enter other industries to handle rev up supporters. Most times novel markets are extra wanted like stocks.

78) - You should score in the jewelry trade. Gobs of stores extend niches to heighten more client. Consistently oddball industries are less aggressive like toy bracelets.

79) - You can exploit the language niche. Several services experience new markets to help boost their site viewers. Various times strange niches are less cutthroat like the English language.

80) - You might contribute in the landscaping market. Thousands of product venders attach to more industries to attract extra hits. Regularly secondary markets are less aimless like flowers.

81) - You could start in the career/jobs industry. Umpteen retailers research more niches to increase their overall readership. Several times sub industries are less unsteady like job sites.

82) - You should grow in the make-up specialty. Piles of establishments appear in new markets to improve their click through rates. Periodically deeper niches are less contesting like lipstick.

83) - You can expand in the manufacturing market. Numerous web sites complement other industries to get more JV partners. Numerous times fresher markets are less patchy like assembling.

84) - You might flourish the occupation trade. Crowds of employers get in extra niches to inspire more sales. Multiple times new industries are less irregular like plumbing.

85) - You could multiply in the men/woman niche. Multiple marketers commit to fresh markets to intensify their web site viewers. A lot of the latest niches are less shaky like sex.

86) - You should amass in the real estate market. An array of storefronts try more industries to speed up their conversions. Repeatedly news worthy markets are less sporadic like condos.

87) - You can make a buzz in the movies industry. Groups of shops access niches to improve their open rates. Sometimes distinct industries are less uneven like horror movies.

88) - You might become rich in the religion specialty. Surges of corporations add bonus markets to maintain more contacts. Frequently proven niches are less risky like prayer.

89) - You could become powerful in the marriage/weddings market. Herds of executives add on industries to make extra colleagues. Many times modern markets are less uncertain like receptions.

90) - You should model the nature trade. Bunches of managers align new niches to sell to more shoppers. Occasionally current industries are less inconstant like nature walks.

91) - You can retail in the neighborhood niche. Many proprietors alliance in other markets to maximize their web site browsers. Most times undersized niches are less viable like security.

92) - You might vend in the night life market. Almost all ownerships bond together new industries to market to more customers. Consistently long keyword niches markets are less crowded like clubs.

93) - You could get branded in the coffee industry. Plenty of distributors union in more niches to motivate new buyers. Various times up to date industries are less crammed like flavored coffee.

94) - You should deal in the exercise/fitness specialty. Various enterprises engage fresh markets to multiply their clients. Regularly, brand new niches are less full like sit ups.

95) - You can produce in the outdoors market. Tons of stores pact into industries to obtain more web site linkers. Several times descriptive markets are less overcrowd like fishing.

96) - You might do commerce in the parenting trade. Millions of services network in other niches to get new acquaintances. Periodically weird industries are less swamped like disciplining.

97) - You could do business in the paranormal niche. Some product venders link to more markets to sell to new connections. Numerous times micro niches are less packed like ghosts.

98) - You should triumph in the pregnancy market. Lots of retailers line up extra industries to preserve their revenue. Multiple times smaller markets are less loaded like nutrition.

99) - You can become wealthy in the people industry. Oodles of establishments joint venture in more niches to prolong their royalties. A lot of more targeted industries are less stuffed like Americans.

100) - You might be the top in the pets specialty. A number of web sites tag team markets to protect their income. Repeatedly tinnier niches are more plentiful, like dogs.

HOW TO START A BLOG

Ever wondered how to start a blog and make enough money to quit your job?

With this book You can do it. Tons of people already have.

Start today you too!

(Second Free Manuscript As Bonus!)

By : "Santiago Johnson Smith"

TABLE OF CONTENTS [BONUS 2 – FREE BOOK] - HOW TO START A BLOG

Blog Basics

Step 1: Consider Your Theme

Step 2: Giving Your Readers What They Want

Step 3: Choosing Your Platform

Step 4: Choosing Your Content

Step 5: Promoting Your Blog

Step 6: Social Networking & Book Marking

Step 7: Tying it All Together

Blog Basics

A blog is sometimes called web log or weblog.   At first, they were used as a personal place, for collecting links, sharing commentary – but now; they are a valid and VALUED form of communication for business people of all types. From the basics of blogging, to the intermediate areas – such as social bookmarking, and article marketing, to the advanced techniques using auto responders and more, there's something for every affiliate marketer to put into motion.

The great thing about blogs is that people read them for fun and for information – in fact, blogging is one of the few areas of the internet that covers business, pleasure, networking and play.

They do for your company what face to face marketing could only do in the past – they provide you with a real, interesting connection to your readers – personalised contact, and information about your company that will allow them to empathise, and discuss your most important points, and anything that ties in with hot button topics and your business.

Blogs give your readers and consumers a chance, not only to read and connect with you, but a chance to comment and discuss with you, and your team, the information that you're sharing – allowing them to further relate to your message. And a consumer that relates to you is a customer in waiting!

Our guide covers the very basics of blogging – it skims into areas that you'll possibly never have heard of – and cover them so that you can employ them in seven days – or less.

Step 1

Starting a blog is as simple as finding a space online to write – and the time to write.

To start though, you'll need to work through a brief list of steps to create your space.

Before you even consider your blog though, you have to think about WHAT you're going to blog about. It's important to stop and think about your blog, before starting it because, to be quite honest, without purpose, blogs are pointless. And this pointlessness will dilute your message considerably.

So, you need to think about what you're writing and why. Consider your theme – and then build some keywords around it, because for the first little while, you should try to include at least some of them in every post. You'll get archived in all of the right places that way, which will lead valuable NON COMMENT generated traffic to your blog. You'll also be commenting on blogs similar to yours and hopefully, generating more traffic based on the links you leave.

You can choose your topic, keyword, and theme simply by considering what, in connection to your business you're an expert in. Once you've looked at that, you can decide whether it's profitable, or viable to pursue it. If not, look at a related area that you can cover – your blog should always relate to your business choices, and give you interested traffic. Having said that, your blog isn't a free advertising system and nothing more – you've got to remember that people will be turned off by blatant advertising.

Choosing your keywords

Keyword Research

Keyword research is relatively simple – you can undertake basic research at

https://ads.google.com/home/tools/keyword-planner/

You can use this to research your general keywords – and check on their general profitability, if you're using CPM advertising. You might not be – but most blogs make a residual income from Adsense or similar, and it's not something you should overlook, for your long term stratagem. Niche blogs can earn well.

Once you've found a profitable overall keyword, you'll need to check out your competition :

https://www.wordtracker.com/

Though considered less effective now – it's still a good tool for finding your competition levels. You'll be able to assess your competition – basically, you're looking for a niche that's either tiny, if it's narrow, or large, if it's broader. Your narrower niches can only support a tiny amount of blogs – whereas the broader your definition, the more your niche will support – but the flip side to that, is that you've got more competition.

Once you've worked out your profitability, and competition, you can also use the keyword search at Overture to evaluate your other keywords (and get an idea on where to start blogging from).

You can place that information in a spreadsheet for reference – or use programs like article architect to extend on your research (affiliate link for article architect)

Once you've made a list of your keywords – and paced them into a spread sheet, you can take your research a step further. Article architect does it for you, but if you've not got that piece of software, or a similar one that researches keywords, you can do it manually.

Open up both Google and Yahoo, and start plugging your keywords into it – at the top you'll see a listing 1 of (a number) – you can then divide your 'competition' number by the total of your searches (a number) – that will give you a rating for that keyword – and the keyword with the 'best' ratings are the ones you'll probably want to focus on.

Article architect does this automatically – highlighting the 'optimum' keywords – and there are other pieces of software will do the same.

The reason you're doing this is to see where your keywords will have the best chance of ranking – you'll be able to find the best place to 'position yourself' this way.

Keep those keywords handy – you'll need them when you start writing content.

Got your keywords? What do you want to blog about?

Once you've got your keywords, you'll have an idea, at least, of the profitable areas of your niche that you can take advantage of. You'll be able to choose an interesting niche – for both you to write in, and your prospective readers.

You'll find that you can narrow it down pretty easily based on what you've got on your keyword lists – and what YOU feel like you want to write.

While its important to work out what you want to do with your blog, based on your view of profitability, it's also important to remember that working based on keywords alone is a sure fire way to build an impersonal, and possibly unmotivated blog for your readers.

Step 2

Look at what you're ABOUT to do from a reader's perspective

One of the more important actions anyone creating or 'cleaning up' a blog can do is look at what you're doing or about to do from the perspective of average Joe reader.

Average Joe doesn't care about profitability. He doesn't care that you're optimising to make the most out of PPC clicks. He REALLY doesn't care that you've worked hard in getting your information into the search engine – and in front of them.

ALL he cares about is what they are looking for – and they are hoping that YOUR site is the site that will provide it.

Average Joe will remain on your site and read ONE POST in for anywhere up to 30 seconds. They might then click on your PPC advertising – they might sign up for your newsletter – they might read more of your posts (yes!) or, if your site doesn't live up to what they were expecting – what they were looking for, they'll click away, either back to the search engine, or to their next option from the search engine.

Blogging isn't just about eyeballs on your page – it's about eyeballs on your page, and comments in your inbox. People have to have a reason to come back, and the simplest way to ensure that is to ensure you've got a reason for them to WANT to visit your site again.

This stickivity is what makes blogging so tantalising- if you can get it right, your blog will attract Average Joe, Average Jane and all of their friends, because the best blogs get commented on in other places – and shared with others.

So, from a reader's perspective is your blog going to fulfil a) your niche and b) give your readers quality, quantitative content that will either strike a controversial or empathic chord with them, giving them something to comment on.

Give Your Readers What They Want

Studies suggest that there's up to a quarter of the internet reads blogs – that's a lot of eyeballs. And on top of that, another study suggests that there's two blogs founded every minute. Two blogs a minute is 120 blogs an hour – and nearly 3000 a day. Take that to its logical conclusions and that's a lot of blogs competing for a less rapidly increasing source of traffic.

More than that though, blogs are competing for a specific NICHE of readers – though its true that some blogs will pull in readers from search engines, blogs still don't have the impact of static sites – and the average internet user may not know HOW to search blogs.

Once you've got the absolute best information in your niche, you can be sure that you'll attract the right kinds of traffic, and that they'll attract MORE traffic by referencing you on their sites – bookmarking you, and more.

Blogging is all about the reader – ultimately, its not about how well you position yourself, or how strongly you optimise your site – though you can bookmark yourself, and generate a certain amount of traffic that way – the best sites have faithful readers that bookmark and discuss the site independently of ANY input from the site owner (you).

The best blogs are one or a mix of tips and advice, hobby or interest discussion, technique and connection. When blogging, if you can make a connection with your reader, then you've won most of the battle. 'Connecting' with your readers is as simple as being personable, and approachable, and giving people a chance to empathise with you.

Who is your reader?

Thinking about what your reader wants to see lets you work out WHO your reader is. Which you'll need later too, to advertise your blog effectively.

So who IS your ideal reader?

Do they have a specific interest, within your niche?

ULTIMATELY, when you know who your reader is, you can plan the creation of a blog that will fully appeal to any readers you attract. If you've planned on whom you're targeting, you'll find it far easier to write content that will continue to satisfy your readers, whilst giving you room to evolve and plan more content as you grow.

Got all of that sorted out?

Now you can move onto the technical stuff!

Step 3

Choosing your platform

There are several major platforms to blog on, but for simplicity's sake, we're only going to focus on three options: Wordpress (self hosted), Wordpress (hosted) and Blogger. All three give you strong, steady options to blog from, and all three are easy to configure – and best of all, all three should integrate with any structure you've already created or are planning to create within your business.

You may find, however, that you can't integrate the self hosted Wordpress with your site, but you should find that you can find a complimentary template on most good self hosted Wordpress blogs.

Wordpress – self hosted

By far and away, one of the most popular options for anyone that is serious about their blogging, the self hosted Wordpress option. You can install your blog anywhere on your site, and its completely within your control, which means YOU can choose what you'd like to have running – an important feature if you're looking to add the ability to do things like email the information to people, or polls. Or your own advertising in some cases.

By far and away, the easiest way to install Wordpress is via Fantastico – most cpanel hosts offer both Fantastico and the ability to install up to date Wordpress. Otherwise, you can find instructions online at **https://wordpress.org**
You can choose your own themes, your own plugins – and modify it in any way you see fit.

Wordpress (hosted)

Hosted Wordpress is a secondary option for anyone whose hosting won't support the Wordpress self install options. You can grab blogs from lots of places, but places like **https://wordpress.com** won't allow you to run a commercial blog.

Hosted Wordpress blogs will only ever offer the very basics of WordPress blogging – you can't control the themes on offer, which means you can't choose a specific theme – unless it's already installed on the site. The same applies to plugins.

Blogger

Blogger is a Google owned blogging system, and is highly popular with non tech savvy people. It gives you a basic frame to build on – and is less flexible than either version of Wordpress hosted blogs.

However, Blogger is a great option if you really don't want to modify anything to do with your blog, other than the theme and possibly add some surface widgets.

Blogger also lets you archive your blog on your own site, giving you all of the benefits of self hosting with none of the update headaches.

Ultimately, there are more software options for your blog – such as Moveable Type (perl based) and Typepad (hosted, by the same company that offers Moveable Type and Livejournal). Moveable type is not free for commercial purposes – another one that isn't free, but is a really solid blogging package is Expression Engine – again, you'll have to make sure that you get a valid licence for it, for the purposes you want to use it for.

What about CMS's?

I'm not recommending any of the CMS based systems, despite the fact that you can use them to build really nice, really strong blogs; you can't use some of the nicer features of blogging that you really need to take full advantage of, to get the most out of your efforts.

Most CMS systems don't have tagging protocols, track backs and pinging - though they have ways to leave comments per article or post, you'll find that they are lacking for full featured blogs.

All of the options will give you a blog that you can build a solid base from, but of course ultimately, where you want to build your blog, be it on your own website or via Blogger (to archive on your site) or hosted with another site, you'll have to stick with what you choose – purely for the fact that you're going to be promoting it – and the last thing you want is to move on after a couple of weeks cause you've played with the others and discover you prefer one over the other.

There is NO HARM in testing them all out first and getting comfortable, if you've never blogged – or haven't explored for a while. Wordpress (self hosted) is easy to install 'vanilla' (no plugins or themes) via Fantastico – just follow the instructions presented and it'll install a simple Wordpress install in around three clicks.

Once you've gotten comfortable you'll need to decide on your theme – you'll also want to pick plugins for Wordpress, play with certain features in Blogger, and add widgets in other programs. We'll cover the plugins and other features for Blogger at the end of the book – for the moment, all you need do, now, is to find a theme you're comfortable with.

Picking a theme

Most people that found blogs have great plans – they want to write interesting content (that makes them money for their effort) and they want to be THE site that people come to for their information.

Most people don't consider what they want their site to look like though. Whether this is a deliberate oversight or if they just don't know what to do with their theme, it's probably one of the biggest 'beginner' mistakes that anyone can make.

Blogger comes with lots of pre-installed themes – or you can add your own CSS to it, to give it your 'unique' look. Its important to at least personalise any theme you choose be it on Wordpress(self hosted) or Blogger – its not possible on hosted versions of Wordpress, or at least, not as easily. There are customisable options on Wordpress.com but they cost money and they are still aren't as flexible as you can have on your own site, so aren't as customisable as you really need to present a professional image for yourself and your blog.

There are many themes that you can choose from – and it can kind of be like decorating your first house – lots of fun, but very wearing!

Wordpress:

https://wordpress.com/themes
https://nicepage.com/wordpress-themes
https://athemes.com/collections/free-wordpress-themes/
https://www.templatemonster.com/it/temi-wordpress-gratis/

All of the above sites allow you to use their themes for free, though its well worth checking the licences – some are completely open – others are restricted simply to personal use.

You can also buy templates from professional designers – or look around and see who other people are using. It's a fair bet that your colleagues or favourite blogs will have designers to recommend highly.

Blogger

Unsurprisingly most Blogger template sites are actually hosted ON Blogger, so you've got a vast array of free blog themes.

https://sites.google.com/view/free-blogger-templates/

https://colorlib.com/wp/free-blogger-templates/

https://btemplates.com/

The final site also contains a lot of wonderful tips outwith the scope of this guide, about how to add more features, such as web albums and forms.

Themes are easiest described as the thing that 'skins' your site to look different – more than that though, your theme controls ALL of the appearance of your blog – it's not just the wall paper on the walls, but the walls themselves in some cases.

Step 4

Blog content

Putting the cart before the horse?

Writing for the web isn't a case of collecting your ideas and then putting them online – and blog posting especially is a hidden and deceptively simple looking 'art form' all of its own.

Before you actually write one word of content though you need to think about what you're going to say. You should have your keywords organised into some sort of coherent list – and you should be weeding out the ones you're not interested in using. Once you've done that, you need to sit down and plan down your blog. You need to plan at least 20 posts and choose some sort of posting schedule.

Once you've planned your content, you can start writing your posts. In the case of WordPress, you can queue your posts as you are writing them, giving you the additional advantage of being able to post series and have them ready to go, without losing your flow. If you're using blogger, you should still write your posts as you can then simply copy and paste them into your blog on the day you want them to go live.

We always recommend that you stay at least three posts ahead of your posting schedule – that way, if you hit a dry spot, or find yourself too busy to post; you've still got 'emergency' content on tap, till you can re-evaluate.

What should a blog post BE?

Blog posts should follow one of a few formulae, but before you look at them – you should probably consider what they can and can't contain – there are a couple of 'no no's' in blogging.

First and foremost – your blog should be advertising light, if it contains any advertising at all. People don't want to talk about your latest and greatest advert – they want to read about your opinions and thoughts in your niche – they want to know that you DO actually know what you're talking about, and most importantly, they want to discuss, not be sold to.

This means that though your blog will do the job of promoting your product, you have to do it without being blatantly, obviously advertorial.

You CAN write about products – talk about why you're so passionate about them – their features, the things that make you want to use them – or the services, or problems they solve.

You also don't need to just WRITE – you can upload pictures, podcasts (audio), video, multimedia – in fact, the more interactive your blog is, without intruding on the experience of the average visitor, the more traffic and return visitors you'll get and the more comments your blog will garner.

Writing for the web

Writing for the web is an art form.

You need to use short sentences, with subheadings, usually one per paragraph – those sub headings should be bolded, to stand out, because studies have proven, without a shadow of a doubt that the majority of internet users, especially those with a lower technical savvy than usual, skim read.

They skim read because we've been conditioned to believe two things about the internet: there's a lot of good information out there – but it can be incredibly hard to find, even on 'trusted' sites. Google's quality, page rank and duplicate content algorithms go a long way to helping to sift the dross from the perfect, but we're still left with people gaming the system, or worse, not being able to clearly state what we, ourselves are looking for.

Back to Average Joe for a minute. He doesn't know how to use boolean operators, in fact, it sounds too complex maths like to be of any interest to him, and many internet users don't search for things as much as ask Google questions.

Keyword searching is a really good technique to learn, but for most people typing in short phrases, or whole questions, is the way to go, complete with punctuation.

Depending on the sophistication of the software in question, they might get exactly what they are looking for, but the same studies that suggest people skim read, also tell us that people really don't understand how to get the most from the internet.

It was best summed up in the X-files – the truth is out there – but where?

Skim reading users do have their advantages – internet writing doesn't need to be tight – just on one (tiny) topic. Blog posts can cover one tiny minutiae of a subject and then head back, stating it differently, another day.

There is one exception to this rule – when the situation or post doesn't warrant that style, don't use it. It's easy for someone to suggest that you blog using subheadings, but if you're blogging about yourself and your family, you might find it very hard.

Blogging is ultimately about YOUR BRAND and YOUR STYLE, so use it well, and you can't go wrong.

The most popular blog post formula

Blogging has fallen into several styles, like articles in newspapers and magazines. You can write and choose to use several different formulae, but ultimately, you have to find a way, and a style of writing that is comfortable for you.

The most common and most responsive way of blogging is 'problem – solution'. You take one common problem or current trend, or newsworthy topic and you 'solve' it.

Solving it can be as simple as providing your opinion, showing where you stand on any given issue, or it could be offering an actual solution to a problem many of us encounter.

Problem – solution or 'action – reaction' blogs are very popular with a vast majority of readers, but aren't without their inherent problems.

For a start, if you're 'solving' a current newsworthy item, although you are giving people a view of the fact that you are, in fact human, you'll also find that unless you are being very careful about expressing your views, you're going to upset someone, somewhere along the lines.

This can be a good thing – being of conviction in what you're saying not only gives you the authenticity that most blogs lack, for fear of stirring up trouble, but will also promote conversation – but not all of the conversation you promote will be positive.

You have to take the good with the bad and accept that no matter what you do, you'll always ruffle some feathers – just like in real life.

Another type of highly popular blog post is the review.

It's fairly straight forward to write a review post, but you've got to be careful. If it doesn't fit with the theme of your blog, you'll find that it actually damages your overall traffic. Your blog should always be laser focussed on the niche you want to talk about, and related areas to the niche. You can't go off topic!

Another type of post is 'a list' – lists of the ten most popular (x)'s.

(x) reasons why (y) is the only option/ a very bad idea

(x) reasons why you should/should not do (y)

(x) life saving hacks.

The highly popular blog, **https://lifehacker.com** is full of these tips and tricks – an article centred on solving a problem. The problem may not be implicitly stated, but instead touched on in general terms, but the solutions are always bang on the money, and that makes this blog a must read.

Its style is easy to emulate too. What problems does your niche have – are there several solutions (that you know of?) and can you express them in simple terms?

The final type of post that is very popular and easy to write is the feature – features can be one article, or several long articles, with links to each other. They should cover something important and be packed full of information. Keyword rich, you want your readers to come away feeling like they've really learned something, and search engines to come away with a whole new platter of wonderful content to add to their indexes.

The art of writing itself

Ultimately, you have to remember that though some blogs are founded for personal gain, if you're working on it to make any sort of income at all; you need to consider that your blog is a marketing project. You're either marketing the content, your company, or in some cases, yourself.

Once you've gotten your head round that, you'll also understand why you can't use slang, or make spelling or grammar mistakes, but more importantly, you'll realise that blogging might be the one 'voice' or face you present to people, so you'll need to offer a consistent, interesting brand.

There are specific, specialised types of post that work well with blogs from an internet marketer's point of view – like information about your company. Go beyond FAQ's and contact information – and share the nitty gritty about your operation. Make your blog readers feel like they are getting in on a secret of some description – or share something that wouldn't ordinarily be online – such as your motivation for going into business.

You can also recommend other marketers that you like, without appearing too fawning, if you're honest. Talking about experience is a sure fire way to improve on both your customer image, and your professional image.

You can also....

Use your blog to archive articles and other freebies for your company.

More importantly than that though, always ensure that you've got somewhere in your blog for people to sign up to your mailing list. Giving them the option to do that will also mean that you've got multiple traffic streaming to and from you blog, and though it seems odd to set up like this at first, people ARE more likely to sign up for your newsletter (with and without incentives!) if they like what you're saying on your blog.

As an extra bonus, you can 'tie' your blog feed to your auto responder, giving people the option of signing up to receive your posts by email – thus negating the need to come to your site until you post – we've covered that in the 'advanced' section of this book.

It has been suggested that there's a definite link between people that sign up for your newsletter, and people that comment on blogs attached to newsletters – and these people are the ones that are interested, interactive readers. They have a vested interest in commenting on your blog.

Style AND substance

Blogging isn't just about providing search engine content, and though its a great way to make connections with your customer base, the most important thing to remember is that shallow content breeds shallow contacts.

What this means is that if you're posting trivial stuff, people that are interested in little more than the trivial stuff will read your blog, and no one else.

Post about the 'meaty' stuff – and you're more likely to not only getting responses, but to gain responses that will help you further shape your content to fit your readers.

Though you will start out with a strong plan, and should try to stick to that as much as possible for the first few months (so as not to confuse yourself or waste the research you did in founding the blog) you should also consider the needs, wants and interests of your readers. Do THEY comment on more of one type of content? Can you write to fit the things they are raising?

Purely from a stylistic point of view, blogging works far better when you're using the active tense (Our newest division opened – we're putting the finishing touches to a launch) rather than the passive (our new division was opened – we've been working on a launch) – passive tense is both flat and doesn't contain energy. Its motionless, and doesn't give the impression of dynamism, which, when keeping a blog is very important.

Speaking of dynamic – ALWAYS be enthusiastic!

Blogging should never be a chore, and if it begins to feel that way, you really need to stop and question WHY.

Blogging is about sharing your passion, your enthusiasm, and your experience with others, and to do that, you've got to believe in what you're writing. If you don't, then how can you expect your readers to enjoy and comment?

If you love what you blog, you'll never work a day on your blog, in your life ;)

Step 5

Promoting Your Blog

Just putting your blog online is not enough. Once your content is off to that flying start (and its perfectly acceptable to found a blog and then backdate a couple (though, not too many!) posts to give your readers something to read. So over days 1 to four, you should have decided what to blog about, created and installed your blog, made sure you've got enough content to last you at least a month and posted it.
Now what?

Well, the long and short of it is, NOW comes the hard work – NOW you have to promote your blog.

Promoting your blog will put it in front of people. Fortunately, there's a myriad of ways to do it, but, unfortunately, they all take time.

Blog Marketing Ideas and concepts

You'll want to make sure that once your blog is developed and in place that its positioned perfectly to capture your market – in doing so you'll find that your blog markets itself.

To start with though, you've got to find your niche – the USP you want to target.

Defining your blog's USP is easy – what sort of reader do you want to attract, and what are they interested in? Does your blog cover it?
That's IT!

Once you've worked out your blog's USP, you can then plan where you want to advertise and approach readers – you'll also be able to track down competitors and colleagues in the arena that your blog. You'll need to know about them to know where best to comment!

Make Your Blog pull people in...

Your blog should, quite literally, mesmerise people and draw them in – interest them in reading about your opinions and information, and most of all, be completely on point for what they were expecting. Your blog should contain as much unique information as you can possibly manage, whether you've rewritten it from PLR or written your content from scratch – it should ALWAYS be unique. You'll avoid Google's duplicate content filter, and better than that, you'll get a reputation for not following the herd.

In the case of internet marketing, this does include ads about launches, but one of the biggest mistakes most bloggers (and mailing list owners!) are making is that they think that they HAVE to share the mailing information they've been given, as an affiliate.

This is a mistake because like seeing the same image over and over again, people will start to block out affiliate based ads – so instead of sharing what you've been given, verbatim, how about writing your own ads?

Its unique content and will interest people far more than flashy music or templates, but having said that, you do need to consider making your blog at least a little memorable. Choose a template that speaks to you on a professional level, but is uncluttered, unfussy, and most of all, interesting and easy to use. There's no point in using a flash template or a FLASHY template if you've got little to no clue how to make it work.

Making your customers aware your blog exists is a bit harder, but not impossible.

Most internet marketers have access to forums, mailing lists and more – so use them to tell people about your blog. If you're lucky, a 'big dog' marketer will see what you're talking about, and link to you – hint, talk about them, though don't say anything untrue! - and you'll probably get some spill over. These 'big dogs' might also consider running a solo ad for you, but you may have to pay for it, and unless you're in exactly same niche as them, or at least one that overlaps considerably, this may not be all that worthwhile for you.

More ways to let people know you exist.

Blogging is an emergent technology – you have to keep this in mind, because if its an emergent technology, so are the ways you promote your blog.

You can promote blogs via link exchanges designed specifically for blogs. There's several of them including:

https://blogcatalog.com
(in this case it only accepts blogs on the Wordpress platform)

Blog catalogues are probably a very good way to get a very small, but very targeted amount of traffic – usually around a similar level to submitting to places like

https://www.searchenginejournal.com/submit-your-site-to-yahoo-and-dmoz-directories/1440/

(a directory for everything online, edited by humans).

Blog link exchanges are less common, despite the fact that there's technology in place, on most every blog, to allow people to share important links, but so far, there's been very little in the way of 'automatic blogrolling' possibly because its so open to abuse.

There are sites though, that run link exchanges specifically for blogs. One of the less typical and highly popular versions of this traffic exchange for blogs is a site called 'mybloglog'.

MyBlogLog as an internet marketing hotspot.

Mybloglog isn't JUST a traffic exchange – it provides 'a return on attention' – it is, in essence the bloggers blog tool. And for an internet marketer, its quite simply a community with leverage.

And as communities go, built around blogging, MyBlogLog is really quite cool. Owned by Yahoo, it does a great job of providing traffic, and growth to blogs.

And therein lies the rub.

You have to be very careful when using traffic exchanges to promote your blogs.

Most PPC based networks (unless you're lucky enough to run your own) frown on it – and some people have reported that they've been banned from ppc using it.

Even Yahoo's oddly.

Having said that, if your primary interest is traffic, you don't need to worry. MyBlogLog gives traffic until you're swamped. And its fairly targeted, as long as you categorise yourself properly.

MyBloglog's community is also a rather interesting place to hang out – you can pick up tips, tricks and find other blogs that are in your niche – again, you need to know where these people are, if only to know what your competitors and colleagues are doing.

Blogging is, when it comes down to it, a community 'thing' – you need a community around your blog for it to be a success, and on the whole, MyBlogLog provides the community aspect that most people need – at least to begin with.

OPB – other people's blogs

I've mentioned, while explaining a lot of this, that you should also know where your competitors are in relation to your blog.

Other people's blogs are also a great way to attract traffic – after all, they've already got people from your niche coming into their blog – the leg work is done – and the really big ones in your niche also have a nice secondary effect.

MOST blogs, when you comment on them, or comment about them and trackback (see the advanced strategies for more information on this!) will provide a link back to your blog, with your comment.

Sometimes its 'no follow' (a protocol introduced by Google et al. to combat spam) which means you don't get 'credit' in the search engines for your link back, but people can still click through to your blog. Its always of vital importance that if you're making a comment that you WANT associated with you that you include a link to your site. Each link has the potential for traffic, either coming to your blog to blast you for your view point (this is still good traffic, believe it or not – if the person cares enough to come over and challenge you, they may stay to read more) or to agree with you, which most times is where you'll pick up new readers from other people's blogs.

The people that agree with you, especially on controversial topics are automatically more likely to comment on your blog – and once someone opens a dialogue, they usually continue it.

That's not to say you should troll blogs to disagree with others. You shouldn't deliberately look for a reason to pick a fight on another blog – in fact, its usually good practice not to argue at all on blogs. If you truly believe the person blogging is presenting a 'fake' point of view, by all means call them on it. Lots of Big Dogs meet people doing that all the time, because its human nature to take a pop at something further up the food chain – but its important that you're doing it for all of the right reasons.

Though controversial conversations are the basis of strong blogging conversations, its also essential that you come away from them looking like a reasonable person, with understandable and approachable way. And as with everything else in blogging the keys to this are reasonable and approachable.

Passion is important, but tempered passion, and reasoned argument are usually the best way to attract people from controversial topics – after all, would YOU feel comfortable talking to someone that screams everyone else down?

Responding to Other Blogs

Controversy aside, there are some important etiquette points to pay attention to when responding to any blog post – or to comments on your own blog: Make sure you understand, fully, what the person is saying. You shouldn't respond to a comment in anger- it'll only lead to escalated tensions, and if something was said in a joking way, however unclear, you'll probably come off looking like the bad guy, even if that's not how YOU meant it. People perceive comments the way they expect the tone to be – so if its out of character for you, it will, generally look far worse.

Once you're ready to respond, you should stay on topic – or at least, start on topic, if you're responding on your blog. If you're responding in the comments area, remember that its a small area and doesn't allow anywhere near as many words as you can fit in a blog post, so if its a LONG response, you should consider taking it, instead to your blog. You should then always link back – blogger ad Wordpress both track these – bloggers calls them 'backlinks' and Wordpress calls them trackbacks (more about effective use of them in the 'advanced' section at the end of the book)

Ultimately, the person that owns the blog gets to decide whether to run your comment. You can't force someone to post your comment and harassing them, again and again, will only lead to you being banned, and possibly named and shamed. Unless this blogger is an unreasonable person themselves, this will only lead to damage.

The bottom line to this is that the more readers you have, the more traffic you have – the more customers you should generate.

Step 6

The social networking and bookmarking debate.

So far, we've touched on the basics of commenting, blog marketing and mybloglog –
now we're going to go into slightly more advanced techniques for garnering readers.

Social networking and bookmarking has grown in popularity alongside blogging and
though not all of them are designed to be used with blogging, most of them are.

Example Site :

https://digg.com

Digg is, quite honestly, the mother ship when it comes to generating traffic from social
networking – you can be pretty much certain that if anyone makes it on Digg, they'll
soon be complaining.

NO server is designed to stream the loads that people see, after becoming a top Digg –
its quite likely that though most people hope and dream of seeing traffic like that, you'll
experience it once and think twice about ever attempting it again!
Digg is a great place to gain readers from certain niches – its a 'geeky' site, a lot like
Slashdot, and is designed to draw attention to the sites that are in those niches, with
worthwhile things to say. They do, however, have a business category, which means
Internet Marketers, with the right slant, can use Digg for bookmarking.

Digging someone is sort of like saying 'I recommend this' – its a global word of mouth script, and is very, very good. Every time someone 'recommends' or diggs you, you rise back up to the top of the front page, giving you a brief chance in the limelight. If you attract more attention there, you'll be dugg again, and again, and again, or you'll sink until someone else diggs you.

There is no time limit on Diggs – no statute of expiry. So its also a great way to get traffic to older posts – and probably most importantly, you can Digg yourself. You shouldn't use your Digg account only for that, but its perfectly acceptable to submit your own site to Digg, occasionally.

The community can't – really – be gamed all that well, because its so vast, but there are ways to cheat at every social bookmarking site – Digg is SO huge though that many people find they just get...buried.

Like every community, it is, in part about friendships – the gaming effect would be really easy if everyone voted for everyone else, but, to be quite honest, most people vote for the stuff that really interests them. So once you hook them as a reader they WILL vote.

There's also no harm (whatsoever) in encouraging your readership, as it grows, to digg you, to bookmark you on delicious, or to add you to other sites – there are plugins and widgets designed specifically for that purpose – just make sure your traffic is voting for the best of your material, and you'll garner even more readers.

The main thing about Digg is its like a snowball. Gain enough momentum and people will continue to vote for you and you'll keep popping right back up to the top.

Step 7

Tying it all up

The seventh day to blogging is a relatively short one – is everything you're doing, working so far?

You won't be able to evaluate traffic, but you should have a comfortable grasp of what you're going to be doing with your blog, and possibly a few fledgling commenters'.

From here on in you should be scheduling regular posting, and regular interaction on other blogs, in communities and forums, and of course, most of all, planning a strategy for continuing the building blocks you've started.

You won't know – yet – where the best bookmarking sites for you are – nor will you be able to decide whether your keywords are appropriate as yet. You WILL, however, know how easily you've found your first week, and you will be able to adapt your project overview accordingly.

You should also decide at this point, where you want to focus properly. Do you want to post daily – and can you commit to that? DO you feel posting less often will allow you to build a stronger, fluff free blog, without over committing? OR would once a week be enough?

Whatever you decide, after the first week or two, you NEED to be consistent. You should find a routine to settle into and then work towards continuing that schedule for as long as possible.

It IS possible to make money from a blog, but those blogs are at the top of their field, and this is simply because they are the best in their niche, blogs wise. As long as you aim for the best quality you can possibly produce, comfortably, you can't go wrong. It may take you a while to attract traffic, but if, in a month, you're still struggling to bring people in, you should review that side of your blogging.

While great content is the cornerstone of the best blogs – they also have a certain amount of focus on traffic driving. At critical mass (when that traffic brings in its OWN traffic) you can relax a bit on that side, but it takes a while to get there.

You should always keep an eye on what works, and what doesn't though, because eliminating that will leave you with a leaner, stronger blog than people that don't pay attention to these things, giving you a definitive edge over your competition.

And beyond?

One month on.

Is your blog outperforming your expectations?

Every marketing strategy needs reviewed every once in a while. You'll need to tweak, to adjust, and most of all, lose the bits that you're getting nothing from.

Step One: Keep Track of Your Blog Results

Tracking your blogs stats is as simple as ABC.

First though, you've got to work out what you want to track. Do you want to track your traffic? Do you care more about comments? How about what you're earning…

Primary goal – traffic

Keeping track of your traffic is as easy as finding a stats program you like and using it. There's a great one built into cpanel called Awstats, or you could use

https://analytics.google.com

Either way, you have to understand how to read the statistics.

Awstats is reasonably easy to understand – the most important two numbers in it are the unique visitors and your page views. You might also want to see who is bookmarking you – in the sense of coming back to visit you using a simple 'bookmark me' function in their browser.

Bookmarking beyond the simple 'favourite' concept.

Favouriting a site, or bookmarking it, is the act of saving the URL in a list that you can then access from a menu in your browser. But in recent years there's also been another way to bookmark a site – and that way is interestingly, to drive boatloads of traffic to your site, if used correctly.

Its most important to remember that this form of 'bookmarking' was initially based on the browser based lists we keep on our own pc's – designed around allowing you to 'share' your favourites with others.

And then sites like Digg, Technorati and Delicious sprung up, giving people a broad range of ways to mark out the best items in another blog – sharing it, with everyone that's interested in the niche of the bookmarked blogs. If you're using social bookmarking, you should also try to keep track of roughly how well it's working out for you – how many 'diggs' you're receiving, how much traffic its referring in. You should be able to see that in your stats too, by looking for url's that refer from the sites that you're bookmarked on. If your website stats are doing their job, they WILL track this.

Once you know how well your traffic is performing, you can decide which content is driving the BEST traffic. If you've got a goal for your blog, be it making money, referrals, or simply driving traffic to your other site, you can use your traffic (and affiliate stats/earnings) to find out which posts are drawing the most traffic and work on extending on those results.

One month in you should have several 'cornerstone' posts that define the whole concept of your blog – giving your readers several strong posts that give both the tone and nature of your blog. These cornerstone posts should be among your strongest performing posts, or you should work on making a couple of stronger ones. These cornerstone posts can also be used, one month in (to give them plenty of time to index in search engines), as articles in sites like **https://ezinearticles.com** – giving you even MORE traffic coming in from relevant sites.

Advanced techniques

FeedBurner

FeedBurner is a great way to add additional options to your site, not limited to subscription boxes, portable feed results, reposting of your information (for example, syndicating your articles is possible just by giving people your FeedBurner code. Their site updates automatically, and you control where they are clicking through to if they are interested in what you are saying in your articles. Its win – win).

FeedBurner was recently bought out by Google, giving you several amazing new options – including opening up their Pro services. Most people use a lot of the FeedBurner functions, so its highly recommended that you grab your own account and explore.

Advanced techniques with FeedBurner also include the ability to 'fix' feeds so that they are readable, and track your feed stats.

Once you've set up your feed in FeedBurner keep the URL handy.

Aweber

If you've fed your Blogger atom feed through FeedBurner this will also work, but Wordpress has feeds that work well with one of the most amazing things that Aweber offers for bloggers, and one of the main reasons I use Aweber.

Aweber has a facility that allows you to attach your blog feed to your email list, giving you the opportunity to email your list the instant you update your blog. This is a great way to automate some of your posting process. And all it takes is filling in a form in Aweber, and putting a subscription form on your site. Not so advanced really.

You'll also be able to set up a template for your posts at the same time – you can choose one of dozens of templates that can compliment your site.

There is in fact, only one caveat to all of this.

If you post multiple times a day, you run the risk of annoying people – and if you don't post enough, your 'newsletters' may not be issued often enough. So you've got to set it up to post at regular intervals, which is where this gets slightly complicated.

Optimal posting is once a week – BUT...if you've got time critical information, this might not work out well for you.

So, you need to work out how to get Aweber to send out an email once a week – if your average posting schedule is three posts a week, set it up to post your information every four posts – add one to your week's post UNLESS you only post once a week – in which case, set it to send once per week.

You'll also still be able to send 'broadcasts' announcing any time critical information – and you'll STILL be able to set up your auto responses to your list – effectively offering you 'triple duty' on your autoresponders.

Other autoresponders may not offer this service so you'll need to check with them.

If your business is more list driven than blog driven, you can also take your list and post it to your blog. You'll need to find a plugin that works with your program – and this does not (as far as I'm aware) work with Blogger.

Trackbacks

There are more ways than one to pay regard to a good blogger – if you're linking to – or someone is linking to you, MOST blogs will track this. Its called 'tracking back' – or backlinking in blogger – or, sometimes even pinging.

It is the art of linking back to a blog that you've read, and referenced – but more than that, its a way to get an effortless link BACK from a blog that YOU read, as long as they accept trackbacks.

Its an advanced technique, because you can't just 'trackback' to from any post – its important to choose only one, two or at a maximum, three blog posts to link back to.

When linking back, you have to use a special link, in the case of WordPress, its simply got 'trackback' on the end.

You use the 'regular' link in the post – this 'regular' link would be exactly the same one as you use to access the single post – you then put /trackback/ on the end of this, and place it in the box designated trackbacks.

As far as I'm aware, Blogger has no option to do this, but might automatically post them.

No matter what you do with your blog, you'll always find that you can get more traffic, more interest, and more eyeballs to your site with a blog.

And no matter how you work on your blog, if you follow our pattern, you'll find that in a month you can make a huge impact on your website.

"To Your Greater Success" !

Email List Building

(For Your Blog)

How To Generate Leads. Many Strategies To Grow Your Email List Quickly. A Step by Step Guide For Beginners To Launching a Successful Small Business.

By : Santiago Johnson Smith

(Third Free Manuscript As Bonus!)

TABLE OF CONTENTS [BONUS 3 – FREE BOOK] - EMAIL LIST BUILDING:

Description

Tired Of Looking For New Customers & Yearning For Residual Income Streams?

Discover How YOU - Or Anyone - Can Quickly & Easily Create Your Very Own Recurring Income Generating Asset Online...

Allowing YOU To Increase Profits From Your Repeat Customers While Building Your Own Expert Status & Credibility In The Process!"

Dear Internet Entrepreneur,

Perhaps you're here because you are still seeking the *right answers* for your Internet business and you need them fast... or perhaps because your business is still really struggling for success.

Let's work together on changing all of that today!

You probably already know the secret to creating recurring riches online... You know, the one that allows you to make money at will and pull in sale after sale, just like clockwork?

Yep, you have probably guessed it: it's having a responsive mailing list.

You can build your own database of prospects... and then build a relationship with them so that they *want* to say subscribed to your list.

You can remind them about your main product that you are selling on your web site... and invite them to return for another look. You can make important announcements so these prospects can visit your site **and then, sell them even more of your products!**

These are just some of the ideas, but you get what I mean, right?

"But It's Often Easier Said Than Done, Isn't It?"

Well, that's list building for you. It's only easy to do if you know the techniques that really work.

Quickly And Easily Build & Grow Your Online Mailing List For Maximum Profits!" And I leave NO stone unturned in this section... because I want you to be able to absorb and USE these valuable tactics right away!

Discover 6 totally different and unique strategies that you can easily execute right now and build your mailing list from scratch! It doesn't matter if you have only a few hundred subscribers or even 0 - these methods can be carried out right away!

What you get:

* A killer technique that can enable you to double or even triple your list building results using any of these tenderfoot techniques alone!

* How to get TARGETED traffic funneled in from major Search Engines online FREE!

* How to use articles to build your mailing list and establish yourself as an authority figure in any niche of your choosing!

* How to earn decent returns from paid advertising online - I show you how NOT to waste money in lousy advertising PLUS show you how to identify paid advertising revenue that really works!

* What it takes to achieve MAXIMUM opt-in rates from your list building campaigns!

* How to drive in laser-focused traffic from popular Search Engines with little investment, MAJOR returns!

* How to use online/offline media to build your database of responsive prospects without having to risk being too "sales pitchy" and resorting to hype in the process!

* Create your vital credibility and then your mailing list through this popular vehicle as used by TOP marketing gurus from around the planet!

* And much more!

Chapter 1: Search Engine Optimization

A Short Introduction...

Thank you for investing your time in this special course, which is likened to the key to your list building success! List building is very, very critical to the success of any business online or offline. And it applies to your success whether you own a small, medium or big-sized business.

Brick-n-mortar companies invest a great effort in collecting prospective leads.

Network Marketers often begin with writing a list of 100 names of people they know. And as an Online Business owner, you should focus on building your Online Mailing List.

Now list building isn't exactly a riddle... as long as you know what to do, and how to do it. Incidentally, that is the aim of this book - to show you how to get started on building your mailing list using multiple, unique and different techniques that add TARGETED leads to your database at as low cost as possible. Yet you can profit wildly in the process.

As more than one technique is discussed in this book, you have my word that at least one or more techniques would suit you - or anyone. Of course, it would be wiser to practice more than one list building technique simultaneously to observe greater results.

Without further ado, let's move on with the first tenderfoot list building technique... Without a doubt, one of the most effective ways in which you, as a website owner, can set up a potential list of clients is to build an email list of those who visit.

SEO (Search Engine Optimization) Introduced By being able to better interact on a more "one on one" platform, you can quickly convert those who would otherwise simply browse around on your website and then leave, into potential sales and money in your pocket.

The profit potential does not stop there though, as with a well-constructed email list filled with people from all walks of life, you can even entice your subscribers to visiting your website more often than they normally would - setting you up to enhance your site's moneymaking ability even more through various advertisements.

So as you can see, the email list is one of the most important tools in any webmaster's repertoire and if you want your online business, no matter what it is, to be as successful as possible then you will need to spend a lot of time perfecting that email list.

Now, you are probably thinking that sure, an email list is great, but let's not get ahead of ourselves - there are many more steps to be done before we can actually start directly marketing to people on an email list.

SEO - Step-by-Step :

First, we actually have to get the visitors to our website before we can even dream of adding them to our mailing lists.

A few years back with the rise of popular search engines like Yahoo and Google, a group of cunning marketers, probably not unlike yourself, decided that the best way to get random people and potential customers to visit their websites was to take advantage of search engine technology.

They figured that if you could code a website and write content for it that designed with the sole purpose of moving that page's status in any given search engine to the top, then they would be able to receive far more visitors than anyone ever thought possible.

In today's web design world, the theory of search engine optimization, or SEO as it is often referred to, is an extremely popular topic among web designers and online business owners from all walks of life - no matter what they are selling or if they are even selling anything at all.

With so many competing websites in your chosen field or niche the only hope that you may have to rise above the seventeenth page of Google is to make sure that your website is as optimized for search engines as it can possibly be.

Because SEO is so popular these days there are hundreds of different websites out there that claim they have the answers to make sure that your page is among the top ten on all of the big three search engines: Yahoo, MSN and Google. However, if you take these tips and tricks on their own, you will quickly discover that there are far too many for you to take in. Perhaps the case is that everyone thinks they have the solution to the SEO problem - but nobody really does, so they just make things up hoping they will attract more visitors to their own websites. Therefore, when scouring the World Wide Web for all sorts of information on how to make sure that your website is optimized for search engines, it is a great idea to compare and contrast the information you find at one website with the information you find at others.

Comparing and contrasting is tedious though, so to get you started, we have already done a bit of the tough legwork for you so you can jump right onto the SEO bandwagon and get your email lists up and running in no time.

Search Engine Optimization Tips :

The first of our comprehensive SEO tips for those looking to establish their own mailing lists is to make sure that your website is as straightforward as it possibly can be.

Anything that deviates from the ordinary, whether it be Adobe Flash integration, crazy layout schemes or the use of dynamic URLs for certain pages under your domain can be disastrous to the budding web designer who is trying to take advantage of SEO for the first time.

Secondly, be specific with the keywords that you select for your website. Far too often, a person who is looking to get into optimization will select a perfectly good keyword but it will be far too general.

What you are looking for are specific keywords, keywords that are searched relatively often but lack the heavy competition of more generic keywords. After all, suppose you put "book" in as your keyword.

That's all well and good, but to be perfectly honest, your website will probably never compete with the likes of Amazon or Barnes and Noble, so be more specific. Consider something more along the lines of "antique book," "first run book" or something like that instead. Finally, be sure to direct your entire website to the optimization cause.

If you want to bring in the traffic (and keep potential customers around for a while) you will have to have great content. That is a no-brainer. But did you know that you can make other parts of your website work for you too? Yes, take advantage of adding your chosen keywords to the header portion of your HTML document, make the titles of your website contain the keyword too, and do not forget to use the "alt" image tags to proudly display your chosen keywords as well. After you think you have a fully mature search engine optimized website up and running, your next step should be to focus on your mailing list. Tweak and tune your content to make sure that it is good enough to make people stick around on your website and offer visitors something that will make them want to join your mailing list.

Promise to give people on your mailing lists essential updates, one time only offers, or whatever else you think is good enough to make them sign up to your email list. Often, the most creative ideas are the most successful, so go wild with your ideas and you will have a successful email list in no time.

Chapter 2: Using Article Marketing

How many different email marketing lists do you belong to? If your mailbox is anything like mine, then you probably have subscribed yourself to quite a few during your browsing sessions online.

Whether the emails that you get are from other businesses that may be able to provide you with goods or services that you simply cannot get anywhere else for the price, for musicians who you like to keep an eye on in hopes that they will visit your city sometime soon or from bloggers who have great articles in your eyes - your email box is probably filled to the brim with notifications that you subscribed to at some point or another.

Now that you are considering moving into the realm of the online business, it is high time that you learn to take advantage of the power of an email list and notification program.

Potential clients and random visitors alike love notification lists, as it keeps them up to date on what you've got going on without them having to visit your website every moment of every day.

People like things to be easy - and that is exactly what an email list is giving them - easy access to information on your website when they want it.

At this point in your career as a blossoming webmaster, you probably do not know too much about the whole web design thing. However, even with your potential lack of experience, you have probably realized that it takes a well-designed website with some killer content to draw people in and make them stick around.

While terms like article marketing and SEO may elude you, it does not take a rocket scientist to realize that you have got to have good, enjoyable, enlightening information on your website to make your guests want to stick around - and one of the best ways to do so is to be involved in an article marketing program.

So What Exactly Is Article Marketing?

Quite simply it is just as it sounds - marketing your articles and taking advantage of articles written by other people to bring traffic to your own website. Because of the definition, there are two very different ways in which you can become a part of the article marketing phenomenon.

Submitting or using:

Whichever method of article marketing your prefer is entirely up to you, although the former is much better way to attract traffic to your website and the latter should only be used in extreme situations.

Thanks to the wondrous power of the article marketing websites, there has never been a better time for you than now to become a better writer. Writing Articles For Business Marketing - You see, in order to be able to take advantage of the amazing marketing potential of submitting to an article marketing website, you first have to be able to write your own articles.

For some people who truly enjoy writing content all day long, this will not be a problem as they will be able to crank out great content in no time and flood the article marketing websites with lots of cool articles that everyone will want to have on their websites - easily getting their names out there so that they can start to establish a comprehensive email list of potential clients.

However, there is that problem that many people face who simply cannot draft an enjoyable document if their life depends on it. If you are one of those types of people, the road to establishing an email list through article marketing will be long and arduous.

Eventually, you will be able to write an article that you deem worthy of submitting to an article marketing website. After some time you may even get a few hits on it and a few unique visitors to your website because of it.

But how much time are you willing to spend on something that may only net you a couple of people on your email list? Instead, why not try hiring a freelance writer.

There are droves of them out there in cyberspace who will work for relatively cheap rates and provide you with decent content (and if you don't like what they have provided you with, you can always edit it).

Although many article marketing websites require that you write the articles yourself, if you have a ghost-writer do the dirty work for you, you can claim the article as your own and nobody will be the wiser.

Submitting To Article Directories :

Once your article writing is finished, it is time to submit your work to an article marketing website. After it has been up there for a while you will start to see people view it and you may even get a few downloads here or there.

It is the downloads that you are really looking for, as it shows that someone found it interesting enough to put it on their website using your name, link, and email address so that people will know who actually wrote the article in the first place bringing your website traffic. Below, you will find a comprehensive list of some of the better article sites on the Internet. There are literally hundreds of sites, but these are the ones you could start with.

List Of Article Directories :

Article City
https://www.articlecity.com

Article Finders
https://scholar.google.com

Articles Factory

http://articlesfactory.com

Articles Network

http://articlesnetwork.com

Constant Content

https://www.constant-content.com

Go Articles

https://ezinearticles.com

How To Advice

http://howtoadvice.com

Idea Marketers

https://www.ideamarketers.com

Morgan Article Archive

http://morganarticlearchive.com

The Ezine Dot Net

https://www.theezine.net

Certificate.net

https://certificate.net

Now, you can also use other peoples' articles on your own website if you must, but remember that you have to provide plenty of links to the original author's website - a risk that can possibly drive people away from your own website before they are able to enrol in your email list.

Getting people onto your email list through an article marketing plan can be tricky and arduous, but for the most part it is one of the more successful methods for establishing a good client base.

A lot of work must be done before you even think about posting that first article on an article marketing site, but once you are through with that all you have to do is sit back and watch as it brings in more and more potential customers to your website.

With each unique visit, there is another chance that person could sign up for your email list. And we all know that the more people on your email list at the end of the day, the more people you can sell to in order to maximize your profits.

Chapter 3: Paid E-zine Advertising

Building a comprehensive email list is one of the most beneficial techniques afforded to webmasters and online business owners these days.

There is perhaps no better way to establish a massive database of potential clients than through an email list that contains the names and email addresses of many who have passed through your site.

However, the problem remains that people must first visit your website before they are able to sign up to your email list, and even the most novice of us know that driving an abundant amount of unique traffic to our website can be a daunting task.

Luckily enough, there are many ways of getting the traffic that we all desire. Some of these ways are free but may take a bit longer to amass hordes of people while other methods require you to pay a fee up front but seem to work a bit faster.

Whichever you decide is totally up to how much you feel you can make in your online business and how much you are willing to spend in an attempt to gain as much traffic - and as long of a mailing list, as you possibly can.

Paid Advertising Explained:

Of the paid for methods of building your own email list and bringing gobs of traffic to your website, possibly the most successful is through paid e-zine advertising techniques.

The e-zine is a relatively obscure topic for most people, and chances are that unless you are really into marketing and advertising you have never heard the name "e-zine" mentioned before now.

Essentially an e-zine is basically an electronic magazine that is published by a particular website.

Different than a mailing list, an e-zine is usually tightly linked to a particular topic or subject, so that everyone who has access to a particular ezine is interested in that one topic.

There are unique e-zines for just about anything out there from how to build a successful website to how to find the best shoes to where are some of the best destinations for people who like to travel by boat.

The possibilities for different types of e-zines are endless, so the first step in any paid e-zine advertising plan should be to find and research the different types of e-zines that will fit into your site's niche.

Sourcing Out For The Best Paid E-zine Advertising:

Once you find a particular e-zine that you feel is the right media for your advertisements, you should contact the owner of the e-zine and see if he is open to the idea of you sticking your advertisements in the e-zine itself.

If the e-zine owner is open to the idea of paid advertising, then you are good to go and you should start creating some advertisements immediately.

On the other hand, if for some reason the owner of the e-zine is not interested in sticking your advertisements in (for any price) then you should simply move on to another e-zine that is also well suited to your business.

Creating Your Own Advertisements:

Now comes the tricky part for any potential paid e-zine advertiser looking to enhance the membership of their budding email list - creating the advertisements themselves.

The ads you make will have to be more than simple content if you want to unleash the full power of a paid e-zine advertisement.

Remember that hundreds, thousands or sometimes millions of people will be viewing the e-zine with your advertisement in it, and if you want a decent majority of those people to actually click your link, visit your website and subsequently sign up for your email list, then you will have to be especially clever with your advertisements.

Even more so if you find that there are multiple advertisers competing with you in the same e-zine issue.

Many people at this point will probably think that their best shot for successful paid e-zine advertisements will be to advertise exactly what their website does, and why someone should pay any attention to it.

Unfortunately, while this may be decent for some people, it is a practice that has proven to be unsuccessful for those looking to build an email list. After all, if a person knows exactly what they are getting from your web service, then why would they want to visit your advertisement if they weren't interested in your services?

That is all well and good if you are selling only one particular product, but you want to craft an email list.

So instead you need an ad that will piqué their interest in what you offer something that will make them want to visit your website, sign up for your email list and come back for more again and again. This is the only way that you will find yourself able to maximize the payout from a paid e-zine advertisement if you are trying to create your own email list.

The Maximum Opt-In Conversion Rate Solution The solution to maximizing email list subscriptions through the use of a paid ezine advertisement is to give the people what they want - something for free or your services in a risk-free offer.

Whatever it is that you offer them for free is totally up to you, and in all honesty it does not really matter so long as you give only a rough idea of what your potential customers are getting for free in the advertisement.

You can give away anything from a free article to free research to a free one week subscription to whatever services you are trying to peddle. Just make sure that you let everyone reading the advertisement that if they visit your website they will be entitled to something cool totally free of charge. Now, just make sure that the e-zine advertisement you have created points directly to your email list sign-up page, tell your visitors that they have to enrol in your email list to receive the free gift and you are all set.

Oh, and be sure that at some point you do actually follow through with giving the people who sign up for your mailing list or you may have a few angry people in the following days. And there you have it, the start of your brand new email list as only paid e-zine advertising can provide!

Chapter 4: Pay-Per-Click Programs

If you want your website, online business or blog to be as successful as it possibly can be, and to be honest - who doesn't? Then what you need is a comprehensive mailing list with names and email addresses of all sorts of people to market your products or services to.

Since most visitors to any given website do not make a purchase on their first browse, it is of the utmost importance that you keep track of as many visitors as you can with an email list. That way, you can more directly market to them later on and convert that marketing energy into sales to generate you profit.

Making the hard sale the first time out is extremely difficult, so use an email list to let the buyers come to you - and then grab them when they are ready to purchase something from you.

The email list marketing tactic works for just about any kind of online (or brick and mortar) business, whether you are selling products, doing custom research for people or writing articles that they can use on their own websites. In order to build an email list that you can later use to solicit your products, you first have to drum up some visitors to your website. This is actually the most difficult part of the task because there is so much competition out there for just about any website.

Even if you think your website is so unique and different from anything else out there, I can almost guarantee you that you will have at least ten other sources of direct competition for your same market - making it harder for people to pick out your website when there are others that may be just as good (in their eyes) as yours. Although search engine optimization and article marketing are viable methods of generating traffic for your website, if you really want to rake in the traffic to build a huge email list, you will have to consider using a pay-for method like pay per click advertising or paid e-zine advertisements.

Sure, neither of these marketing techniques come cheap - but if you can add even a handful of the visitors you get from these campaigns to your email list, then a pay for advertising method will be totally worth it.

Pay-Per-Click Exposed!

Thanks to the success of the search engine business in the past few years, the pay per click advertising method seems to be the best payoff for someone looking to generate traffic and build their own email list. Because so many people frequent search engines like Google and Yahoo each and every day, pay per click advertising is the perfect way for you to get unique visitors to stop by your website - even if search engine optimization techniques have not been able to bump your website up to the first page yet. So, if you are interested in gaining the best benefit for your buck in terms of visitors to your website, then paying Google or Yahoo each time someone clicks on your ad is well worth it.

How It Works:

Each and every time someone clicks on your ad, you will have to pay a small amount of money to the company you purchased the ad space with, but if you are turning most of those visits into sales or valuable additions to your email list, then the fee will be well worth it.

Google is one of the biggest names in the search engine business and their ability to bring in visitors to all sorts of different websites should not be taken lightly.

With well-placed Google pay per click advertisements, just about any web business owner can turn his downtrodden website into a moneymaking bonanza in a matter of weeks.

Thanks to their ingenious AdWords program, Google will be happy to give you a plethora of pay per click advertising space on the results page of peoples' searches to advertising sections on other peoples' websites.

Yes, with a contract with AdWords you can be well on your way to getting visitors left and right. However, as with all things that seem so great, there is a catch with Google AdWords - you have to work long and hard on choosing the right keywords for your website.

The special algorithm used by AdWords only shows a few relevant ads based on keywords, so if you are unsuccessful in choosing the right keywords for the most effectively targeted ads, then you will be left with far fewer visitors to your domain than you though.

The other promising choice for those looking to get into pay per click advertisement as a way to get visitors to their website for email list purposes is to use Yahoo's Search Marketing (formerly known as Overture) service.

Since this service has been around much longer than Google's AdWords, it is much more robust in terms of what you can do with it.

While AdWords is much more focused on targeted advertisements, with Yahoo Search Marketing you can actually target your ads by different criteria - not just by the keywords you have chosen to use. This gives you as an online business owner much more flexibility over who gets to view your ads and when they get to view them.

Now that you have been acquainted with the top two names in the pay per click advertising marketplace, you should be better prepared to make a decision about how you want to go about attracting visitors to your website.

With pay per click advertisements, you do not have to worry about spending money frivolously on ads because you never have to pay anyone until somebody clicks on the ad for your website. Furthermore, with both Google and Yahoo, you actually get to name your own price for how much you pay per click - making pay per click advertising a feasible method of generating website traffic even for those webmasters on a tight budget.

As one final tip for anyone looking to get into pay per click advertising as a way of building an email list, make sure that your advertisement is linked directly to your email list signup page, as you cannot expect people who have visited your website via an ad click to browse around for long.

Chapter 5: The Value Of A Press Release

Building a successful website can be tricky business - especially if you have plans to make that website the crux of your income statements each year.

After all, with so many other websites out there that are probably selling the same or similar goods and services as you, what is there to set your business apart from the pack?

One simple answer should be the contents of your website. People like a nice, clean design for the sites that they frequent and they like to have plenty of enjoyable articles or copy to read that is genuinely interesting to them.

If you are able to supply those two fundamental features you will be well on your way to making your online business thrive. But what if you want to take that extra step to make your website into a moneymaking machination?

There is one simple tool that you can employ if you want to ensure that you will get more people to purchase from you - create an email list that potential customers and current customers can sign up for.

The mailing list allows you to do something that most stores wish they could do: attract visitors and then market products to them on their schedules so the hard sale does not seem so hard to swallow in their eyes.

Even with a small email list you will have a much higher rate of sales than if you were to forgo the email list all together, so what do you say - perhaps it is high time that you create one for your website. Unfortunately we cannot go around and simply collect random names and email addresses to add to our email lists, so it is up to us to first generate enough traffic for our website and then convert those visitors into email list subscribers.

There are tons of different ways in which you can get traffic to come – some ways, like pay per click advertising cost you some money while other like search engine optimization are totally free so long as you know what you are doing.

However, both of these techniques are totally passive. Try as you might, it may take you weeks or months before you actually see any of these techniques come to fruition as actual inquiries on your email list.

Instead, if you want to grab the proverbial bull by the horns and rake in people by the droves right away then you will have to do something a bit more drastic.

Bring In Press Releases!

That something is a tried and true technique that has been employed by businesses of all types for centuries. Known as the press release, you can use this method to drive people to your website almost instantaneously the moment someone picks up and publishes the release.

At this point you are probably thinking that such a technique is too good to be true and would be impossible for a lowly online business owner like yourself – but the good news is that anyone can draft a press release and submit it to many of the major daily publications, both online and print based. All it takes is a little bit of time and some know-how of what you need to include in your particular press release.

Drafting Out Your Press Release:

The first aspect of a press release that you need to concentrate on is the actual content of that release itself. Nobody wants to read some drab, boring press release - and certainly nobody will want to publish it in their periodical, so consider jazzing it up to include a lot of content that people who would be interested in your website would want to hear. Include facts, figures, statistics and even plans of action for what you and your business plan to do in the future in an attempt to get people to check out your website.

Remember: no sales pitch, too! People expect something newsworthy from you. While you should make the content as interesting to your potential customers as possible, it is important not to lie, since chances are that your potential clients will check up on you over time to make sure that you are wholly backing up what you say in press releases with what you actually do. Also, when writing the content, be sure to address your possible clients personally instead of addressing them as some vague demographic as far too many press releases tend to do. This will make the reader feel more at home and will likely make him or her more inclined to visit your website.

Secondly, if you plan on submitting your press release to mostly websites who will publish it, then you should try to optimize it for search engines as much as possible.

Remember that the more aligned your press release is with certain keywords the more it will be read by people who could be your potential customers and subscribers to your new email list, and the better it will be for your business in the long term.

Please though, do not overuse the keywords you have decided to focus on, as it will make for a very dry, boring and uninteresting press release that certainly will not allow you to get the maximum number of visitors.

Finally, once your press release has been written and edited, you will want to find some spots to post it. I recommend these (but there are many more if you 'google' the term):

https://www.prweb.com
https://www.newswire.com
https://www.imnewswatch.com
https://www.pr.com/press-releases

Be sure to get into contact with places that you know will be able to distribute your press release to the masses, but also try and find some avenues of distribution that take advantage of RSS or Atom feeds. Using RSS or Atom will allow your press release to be sent directly to the masses like the top headlines for the New York Times or Google News and is a great way for your business to take advantage of technology in the pursuit for a massive email list.

So there you have it, the basics for using a press release to gain as many visitors to your website as possible. Since you are looking to establish an email list from many of those visitors, be sure to have the link from your press release pointing to your subscription list page, as you do not want people to dawdle around on your website and lose interest before they sign up for your email list. Do this, and you will quickly find that your website will be successful in much less time than you ever thought possible!

Chapter 6: Using Special Reports To Kick Start

Your Campaign Marketing is about contacts, and in today's business world, emails are as valuable as just about any contact you can have. The key, though, is not just to have a list of emails; it is to have a list of qualified emails that you can turn into clients and profits.

Certainly getting a list of qualified email contacts sounds great, but how do you do it? There are a number of ways to get qualified emails, but one of the most effective ways is through the special report.

When used properly, the special report can give you and your business credibility while helping you to build an email list of qualified potential clients.

Take a look at the information below and you will quickly be on your way to building your business through an email list created from a special report.

Creating a Report About Your Subject:

Perhaps the best way to encourage perspective clients and customers subscribe to your e-zine or email list is to provide them with relevant and useful information. Your special report allows you to provide something of value (information) to your prospects without discounting your product or giving anything away.

Before you can start to use your special report, you obviously will need to create one. This is the most important part of the process, because if the report is not put together correctly, its effectiveness will be compromised even if you do everything else exactly right.

Start by considering niche topics that will benefit your prospective clients. If you offer real and useful information, those who read the report will be more likely to opt into your email list in hopes of gaining access to more useful information from you down the road.

If your report is not useful, prospects will be less likely to read the report and even if they do it may not result in the email opt-in even 'sticking with you' and with whom you are hoping to build your email list.

Secondly, research your special report heavily and make sure that your information is rich. Good content will bring opt-ins while bad content will just disgruntle prospects and leave you with a bad report and no emails.

Finally, proofread and edit heavily. Your content should be smooth, well written, and easy to understand. Good information that is easy to understand makes you look good.

On the other hand, good information with lots of errors and that is difficult to understand will may make you look inept. Have several sets of eyes look over your special report before you move on.

Turning Your Report Into A PDF Document:

The next step, once you have written your special report, is to have it converted into a PDF document. PDF files have a more professional look and can make you look technologically savvy to your customers.

What's more, they will look exactly the way you designed them no matter what the hardware or software is that the recipient uses. Converting your special report into a PDF document is simple, so the amount of work you put in versus the payoff is profound.

There are a few ways to convert your file into PDF format, and one way is to find a reliable and free online converter (Adobe.com has one) or you can download a software product to use on your own computer. Using your favorite search engine, you can find numerous free software applications that will convert any printable file into a PDF file. If you are only doing a few special reports, this is the fastest way.

I recommend:

https://www.primopdf.com or https://openoffice.org for the job, but there are several others, as well. There are many options out there, so do your homework and find the one that works best for your business.

The important thing here is to make sure you get a clean conversion and that your special report looks professional and just the way you designed it.

Circulating Your Report:

You have created a special report on a topic that you know about and that pertains to your target clientele. That is great, but now you have to make sure that they are actually looking at the report.

If nobody reads your report, it obviously won't do you any good. So then how do you get your special report circulating and working for you?

First and foremost, make sure it is well known within your company. It should appear on your website as a download and your employees should have links to the download location on their email signatures.

This will give your existing clientele access to the special report and anyone with which your employees have contact: a nice start.

The second way to circulate your special report is to write shorter content that will appear online where your prospects are looking.

Write a small article that leads to the information in your report, add a link to the report at the end, and post the articles on content websites and even message boards. Spread the word through the industry that you have something of value for free.

Finally, create a flier or other print advertising for your special report. Include the location (a link) for the special report and make your flier available at conferences, conventions, and any other event where you may encounter potential clients. Getting the word out every way possible will assure that plenty of eyeballs are finding your report.

Building an Email List from Your Report:

Once you have a useful report with good content, and once you have properly marketed that report so that it is in front of potential clients, you need to get emails from them.

The email list you are about to build is the main reason you created your special report in the first place. So how do you build an email list from your report? If you have put together an effective and valuable special report, then your clients will want to give you their email. Your job is to make sure there is a way for them to do that.

Within your special report, offer opportunities to get more information from you by opting into your email list. Offer an e-zine or other information to potential clients who do so.

Provide links to your company website on most if not all pages of your special report. At your site, make sure opting into the email list is easy to do, convenient, and quick.

If your target sees something he or she likes, it should be convenient to get to your site and to sign up for your email list. Remember that the report needs to stand alone as both an informative special report and as a marketing tool to help you collect qualified email leads.

This is important as you allow the report to be resold and passed along by others in the industry.

A Valuable Tool:

As you can see, using a special report can be a great way to build your email list. What's more, you will find that there are many things you can do to make your special report an ongoing aid in the maintenance and continual building of your list.

Just remember to make the content good, the report valuable, and the opt-in process convenient and you will have a qualified and reliable list in no time!

This Ends Part One...

This pretty much sums up the basic techniques of list building. While there are obviously more advanced list building techniques that you can practice and use for your own, I thought you should know that many a top marketer are making it big online today using even some of these "basic" methods to build their list... to a great extent!

You now know what it takes to build your mailing list from scratch, and I would advice you to test every one of them to see what works best for you. This is because every individual is different.

Therefore there are some methods that would work especially better than the other for you. Are you ready for the 'intermediate list-building' training section now?

Chapter 7: Compound List Building with Resell Rights

As you may well know by now from the last chapter in Ultimate List Builder's Course, creating special reports is a great way to market your business.

You can use those reports to build your credibility, raise the awareness of your company, and acquire qualified lists of emails for potential clients.

In order to truly spread your special report around, which is how you get the most benefit from it, you should look into granting resale permission for the report.

Once you have written your special report, you have to find a way to make sure that people are actually reading it.

After all, getting people to read your special report is the only way to reap the other benefits of writing one.

As you will see, there is a lot to be gained from resale permissions.

In addition to that, it is easy to get started once you have written your special report. Finally, you will see that your email list may just be the biggest winner in the resale permission game.

What is Resale Permission?

You may have heard the phrase "resale permission" before, but it is possible that you didn't know what it meant.

Basically, if you grant resale permission on a special report you wrote, you are giving another person or company permission to sell or distribute your report and collect any profits for themselves entirely.

While that sounds like a great deal for the person to whom you grant permission, it is also a pretty good deal for you and your company.

Of course, first you have to understand how to do it.

How to Give Resale Permission:

Giving resale permission in and of itself is not difficult, but you want to make sure you do it the right way. Remember that you want to make it easy for your special report to get spread around. That means that you need to grant your resale permission the right way.

The best way to get started is with an opening statement that outlines your resale rights terms. Now, for some resale rights, you can offer up minimum resale prices, restricting free giveaways, and even restricting membership site usage.

However, if you are trying to spread a special report to build your business and your email list, then you should consider making your resale rights simple and easy to get.

The easier it is for someone to acquire the rights, the more likely they are to take on your report and start selling and giving it away. When you are trying to expand an email list, you need to make sure that you do add one resale right permission restriction. You need to make sure that the main text of your special report stays unchanged.

That will ensure that links and references to your website or company and thus assist you in growing your list. Overall Benefits of Granting Resale Permission For Your Special Report.

When you choose to offer resale permission on your special report, you can gain a number of advantages. For one, by granting resale permission, you are encouraging others to spread your report. That means more eyes reading the report and about your company.

Secondly, offering up resale permission gives you credibility. As other read the report and it is being resold, you become more of an authority on your subject and, by manner of extension, so does your company.

Finally, you create a viral situation. When you offer easy to get resale permission, you are basically enlisting a large number of people to spread your report one way or another. That just helps the word spread that much easier.

Email List Benefits of Giving Resale Permission:

What, though, does this all have to do with expanding your email list with qualified potential clients?

Simply, when you wrote your special report, you should have done so with proper wording and links so that your opt-ins would grow. With such links, references, and other referrals coming from your special report, you are looking for a way to get that report in front of as many potential clients as possible. So by granting resale permission, you are creating a way to get your report in front of more people.

The more people you have looking at the report, the more people you have getting the opportunity to look for more information with your company and the more likely you are to get people adding their names to your email list. This will help your email list to not only grow, but also to grow with qualified leads. As you can see, there is a lot to be gained by writing a special report and granting resale permission to others for it.

It is one of the most efficient strategies you can use to get your special report in front of as many people as possible. Remember to start with a report that actually has value.

In addition, make sure it directs people to your company website as well as your opt-in email list in order to build a better list of qualified potential clients.

Finally, give permission the right way. Do not overcomplicate things by putting a lot of restrictions on the resale rights. Instead, make it easy for people to acquire the resale permission and they will be more likely to take it.

Remember, you are trying to get your report to spread. You are not looking to make a profit on the report by itself.

So once you have that understanding, you can just allow people to spread your special report to all those potential clients and members of your email list.

Thus if you are looking for a way to spread your special report, check into the granting of resale permission.

You will be glad you did it.

Chapter 8: Using The Ad Swap

Whether you are writing an E-zine or building an email list, your clients are important. Have you already exhausted all other means of getting more email addresses? You may want to consider using Ad Swaps.

This is a way for you to not only to increase your client base, but also gain more revenue from other sources. You may find that something as small as swapping ad's with different companies will give you the boost you have been looking for.

So What Is "Ad Swapping"?

This is actually exactly what the name implies. You swap your firm's ad with another firm's ad. Finding an Ad Swap group is as simple as using your favorite search engine. There are many companies out there that are interested in Ad Swapping.

Swapping your ad with another company can greatly increase your chances of gaining more subscribers. When you swap ads with another company, you will be displaying their ad instead of your own.

This means that your ad must be short enough to work with the company's email layout, but also be informative enough to grab the attention of the reader in hopes to directing them to your website.

Ad Swapping is smart advertising. Many times when individuals are browsing the internet, they may not know what they are looking for, but those that are already subscribed to an E-zine or other list already know what they are looking for.

Using Ad Swaps Correctly:

By correctly choosing the right company to swap Ads with, you will greatly increase your use base. This is because the readers are already interested in what they are reading and see that the Ad pertains to what they are reading and also that it is recommended as a reputable site by the person who supplied the original email.

A simple Ad Swap can bring in double the amount of people that you have now.

Before you even consider swapping your Ad with another person, you need to create a one-line description that will really make readers want to click on your Ad.

The "Ad Headliner" is the single most important part of the Ad. Without it, you are not left with much. The Ad Headliner should not be very long but should contain enough information that grabs the reader's attention enough that they want to visit your Ad. This is the same as Internet Ads.

If there is a lot of text you must read before you figure out what they are trying to bring to you, you most likely wont click on it. For this reason, keep your Ad Headliner short and sweet but powerful.

Sometimes a few words will work best, its up to you to decide the right length that is informative without being long-winded. There are many different companies out there and it's important to make sure that the Ad you get in return will be fit for your client base, and vice versa.

One of the most important aspects to consider when you are looking to swap ads with any other person is how well their content relates to yours.

This just means that if your clients expect information about computer hardware, they aren't likely to click on an Ad that is about horse racing equipment.

This is not to say that everyone interested in computer hardware isn't interested in horse racing equipment, but at the time they are reading your E-zine, they may not really have that on their mind.

The topic of the Ad does not necessarily have to completely pertain to your Email, but it does need to be related. One other point to remember is to find out how many users the other person interested in the Ad Swap has.

Since you are interested in gaining new members, then it is in your interest to only swap Ad's with another person who currently has the same or more number of users. Of course, if you have only five percent more users than them, you can still give them a chance.

Just remember that you are interested in gaining new members, and if your Ad Swap partner has a fewer number of members, then your odds of gaining new members drops significantly.

What if you cannot find a company who shares the same interests to Ad Swap with? One solution to this problem might be creating a survey for your customers with a wide selection of topics for them to choose from.

This will help you understand what other interests they share, and can help you make a smarter decision on who to trade your Ad with.

back from all of your customers, you can safely choose one of the top interests and know that you will be doing your part in relaying traffic to your Ad Swap partner.

Choose your topics wisely though. You don't want to have your topics cover a gigantic area of interests, because finding a company that needs an Ad Swap partner with your particular interests may not want to trade with you if your material pertains to a topic that differs too greatly from the one they cover.

Offering your customers between Twenty to Thirty different interest topics to choose from will give them a nice selection, and make things easier when it comes time to find an Ad Swap partner. Joining an Ad Swap group can greatly increase the number of members you currently handle. It is one of the best ways to get more subscribers to your E-zine or other subscription email service. Be sure that you research each person who you are conducting the Ad Swap with as their content will be displaying to all of your subscribers and you are the one responsible if they supply you with a broken link. Be sure to write a few ad headliners and choose the one that is both minimalist and descriptive.

Without an attention-grabbing Headliner, an Ad Swap is useless. As long as you are sure to check over all of these points you should be on your way to conducting a successful Ad Swap.

Chapter 9: The Magic of Give-Away Events

Building an email list is one of the best ways to advertise the product or service that you are trying to market. This will keep your efforts focused on your target audience instead of to a broad range of people who may not need or want to do business with you.

For example, if your business deals with home improvement information and products, you would not likely appeal to someone who is living in an apartment.

The main purpose of building a large, active email list is to bring in a sizeable amount of active readers who are looking to you for good deals and benefits.

Successful e-zine creators often credit their good fortune with hosting GiveAways, or contests as incentive to get people to join. Of course, once they join they will expect to receive a well-composed and beneficial newsletter or else they will likely choose to unsubscribe.

A new business might not be able to afford to give away free products to subscribers in the beginning, especially without the knowledge of how successful the newsletter will be in bringing in actual profits.

This is why it is a good strategy to find at least one reliable affiliate who you can either trade products with, or that is willing to give you a wholesale price.

List Building Through Give-Away Events:

Before you approach anyone in search of partnership, you should be fully organized and have a sample newsletter ready to present to them.

Be confident and show them that you have the drive to put in the efforts that it will take to make it work. It may take patience and friendly persistence to have anyone agree to take on a risk involving finances.

However, this situation could be very beneficial for both parties. You will have the means to get a customer base built and, if they can supply you with their products to give away, they will build a good reputation and increase earning potential.

If you don't know where to begin looking for a business affiliate, try looking for a successful business of any size that is in the same product category. This could help you bring customers to each other.

You may not be comfortable asking for money or products, but you also have the option of trading equal parts of your products with theirs to give away to subscribers of your e-zine. They may choose to do the same, which would help both of you. Neither of the parties will lose much money considering low production cost to the manufacturer.

Using this strategy to bring in customers will have you making the money back in no time. A simple outline of what to do to find a partner is as follows: propose your strategy for building an e-zine newsletter to potential partners, show them a sample newsletter to gain their confidence, and use your skills of persuasion discuss ways that you could make the most of each of your products and help each other's business.

If they are hesitant and don't seem interested, move on. Anyone who has the ambition to start this type of venture will be able to find a partner who is just as eager to work with him or her.

Do NOT immediately advertise your Give Away.

It is important to wait until you receive the products that you will be sending out.

A formal contract should also be agreed upon and signed because they are a common practice in the business world. Decide when would be the best opportunity to give away a free product to subscribers.

If you do it at the time they sign-up you will risk having people sign up just for the gift and then canceling their subscription.

One way to ensure that your list grows, and remains active, is to require that membership is at least one month old before they can apply for the free gift.

Another alternative is to have a monthly drawing for the items you are giving away. That will keep readers of your e-zine entering each month for the contest.

This will give subscribers incentive and they may even help you by referring friends and family to join. Being aggressive in this situation will not hurt your reputation.

If you already have a great web site, don't hesitate to advertise the Give-Away exclusive to mailing list subscribers on every single page. It can be placed in a spot on the page that will not interrupt the flow of the page, such as the bottom or top corner.

Do you offer a site subscription?

Add a check box to the sign up page offering to automatically add them to the email list also. The free gift should not be the only reason they choose to sign up.

Offer a link to a sample of the newsletter so that potential customers can see the benefits and incentives that they will receive in each email.

You have to be ready to work hard to make people happy and keep them interested in what you have to offer. The double opt-in practice is important to anyone who is building a large mailing list. Anyone with genuine interest in becoming a part of your list will be willing to confirm their request to join twice.

This is your opportunity to remind them to add your address to their white list so that it is not filtered out with spam.

Using only single opt-in signups will bring in a large number but the quality of the list will definitely suffer.

You will either be filtered as spam or have to deal with a lot of un-subscribing from those who were never interested in what you have to offer.

Keep up the maintenance on your list.

Don't be afraid to ask for feedback from your active readers on what they would like to see more or less of.

This will let them know that you are genuinely interested in their business and satisfaction.

A Give-Away is a proven effective way to get a list started, but it is up to the creator to keep the list as active as it is large.

Chapter 10: Investing in Co-Registration Leads

Too often the key to your business working successfully is how much traffic you can drive to your website.

The type of product or services you offer can sometimes limit traffic.

This means not only do your potential sales suffer but so does the growth of your business. One way to improve this traffic flow is co-registration.

This means putting opt-in check boxes on the page where your customers register.

Co-Reg & Opt-Ins - They Go Hand-in-Hand:

Opt-in boxes are places that your customers, or even just those who visit your site, can check to say if they are willing to receive information on similar products, services or e-zine publications.

This allows you to build up an email list so that when you have sales or introduce new products you are able to get the word out to potential clients quickly.

Building mailing lists is an important part of running an online business. But, it is something you cannot necessary do all on own.

There are companies who can help you build mailing lists that will reach customers that will potentially be interested in what your site has to offer.

There are companies who will sell you co-registrations leads to help you build that all important mailing list. But before you agree to buy from them you must be certain that you will get exactly what you need. There are some basic guidelines to shopping around for a good co-registration service. To begin with, the company must guarantee you that the names you are being given are genuinely opt-in names.

The last thing you want to do when trying to bring in customers to view your offerings is to use names that have been collected without the customer's agreement and authorization. Then you also want them to guarantee you that the names have been generated recently.

Co-Reg Tips:

The age of the leads you invest in is a crucial factor. Names that were picked up a year ago will not likely be of any use.

People change their email addresses regularly when they change jobs or move. And, over time their interests change, as well. The products or services they were looking for which are common to your business may already have been bought.

That is what makes 'old' lists an even bigger waste of money.

The other thing to consider is price. The cost of co-registration lists varies from company to company so shop around until you find what you think is the best deal. Do not use price as the only factor, but use it as one of the factors. You want a company that will offer to you everything you need at a reasonable cost. Whether you are building your mailing list to draw people to your e-zine, announce new products or get new names for your monthly newsletter a service that offers you good co-registrations lists will save you time and a lot of work.

If you want a list that can bring you hundreds of names doing it yourself could take months. Getting them from a service cuts that to a matter of days and lets you get back to growing your business. There is no other lead generation resource better through the Internet than this.

If you are looking for a source of co-registration leads finding them on the Internet is not difficult. But you must try to find one that will offer you what you need.

The service at

https://smallbusiness.chron.com/coregistration-marketing-24798.html

seems to have a lot to offer to their potential clients, as do the folks over at List Opt. When checking out any list service, make sure that they offer is a guarantee that you will be satisfied with their products. Also be sure that they offer lists that are generated the correct way; with no contest lists being used to trick respondents into allowing their names to be taken. And it's VITAL that all their names are optin.

They will have co-registration lists that are aimed solely at that one area. This may be any form of product or service. One service that sells co-registration lists like this has them aimed particularly at those who are interested in Internet marketing. Their claim is that those who are on their lists are eager to find ways to make money on the net. So, if that is what you are offering on your website their co-registrations lists are for you. They can be found at Nitro List Builder. This particular company also offers larger lists than most others. They talk of the availability of lists that have from twenty to one hundred thousand contact names. Like the other one they promise their lists will be fresh ones.

Many of the co-registration sites that sell email leads are particular about what kind of businesses they will work with.

They will stay away from hot businesses, gambling sites or sites which reflect an attitude of hate against others. This shows that they are trying to make aim their business at others whose businesses do not hurt anyone.

They are careful to ensure that there will be no duplicate names and that all the leads you get are current. This is a very important aspect of co-registration leads and one that all services that sell these leads promise you.

You can always expect to get a few email addresses that have changed but if you wind up with too many dead leads you should contact the service you have bought from and demand replacements. If the number of dead leads is high they should honor your request. Some services will give you an extra one or two percent on your order to help ensure that you get the right number of goods leads for the money you have paid. Prices vary greatly on co-registration leads. You can pay anywhere from thirty-six dollars for one thousand names to three hundred dollars for twenty thousand names and many possibilities in between! You're Almost Finished With the guide Part Two... There you have it! Both the basics and advanced list building techniques are now as good as at your fingertips. Note though, that you require some substantial list and/or experience to use some of the advanced list building techniques discussed in this course, while others can be done just almost immediately. All in all, they can prove to be very powerful list builders if mastered correctly. It is my sincere wish that these techniques can help you expand your mailing list and in doing so, expand your Online Business Empire even further. See you at the top! (When you are ready for the "hardcore" level, let's get started with the guide Part Three... the last edition in the series... just scroll down!) Bringing Your Online Business To The Next Level Welcome to the last sequel in the Ultimate List Builder's Course series, where you will discover some of the most hardcore list building strategies as used and practiced by TOP Internet Marketers and gurus from around the planet! Now I am going to confess that it's not going to be necessarily easy to execute any one of these Master's Level of list building techniques, as they certainly require more practice backed by experience to leverage on them.

But it is a worthwhile learning journey as these list building techniques has been responsible for income breakthroughs of many an Internet Marketer, some who brought in thousands, potentially tens of thousands of red hot leads in a short time span, some literally overnight! I won't stall you any further as I could almost feel your excitement. Let's move on! Scroll down for chapter eleven... and learn more methods to help you build your list.

Chapter 11: Recruiting an Army of Affiliates

If you are an Internet marketer, one of the keys to a successful business will be your ability to bring potential customers to your website.

The best way to do this is to find a way to build large email lists of these potential customers. One of the most common strategies for doing this is purchasing opt-in co-registration lists.

An opt-in list, as you already know by now, are those where the customer has checked a box on a site saying that they are willing to receive information through their email for different products.

Building, or buying, these email lists are what will make the difference to a successful Internet marketing business. It does not matter what you are offering on your site, products you want to sell or services you are offering, if you do not have the traffic to your site you will not make money. IMPORTANT! You should not purchase lists that are not recently generated or that are not opt-in generated. If you do then you will not add to the success of your business but will find that too many of your leads are cold and you have spent money for very little, if any, benefit to your business.

Affiliate Programs Exposed:

Another way to drive traffic to your site is to become part of an affiliate program. This can be done either by joining an affiliate program that is already showing signs of success or by making one yourself.

Joining Affiliate Programs:

Joining an already established affiliate program has several benefits.

Obviously the first one is that the program is already up and running and so there is less work for you to do and less time to wait for results from the program. You would need to search the Internet and locate affiliate programs that are related to what your product or service is. It would make no sense to sign up to any program if the topic is not close to what you are doing. This does not mean that you should be concerned that you are signing up in a program that is run by your competition.

In reality any affiliate program you join that properly reflects what you are marketing on your website will have other members who potentially are your direct competitors.

This does not matter. Customers will shop around. If what you offer is a better product or service, with better financial considerations the customers will come to you.

This gets others to help increase your business prospects. What you want to do is get the affiliate programs to work for you. In this way you create your own email lists, use ones that you have bought and bring them all together through an affiliate site, which will not only generate potential customers for you but can potentially earn you money as you send customers to other sites.

With affiliate programs, if you join them, then you get commission on their sales. This can be a nice perk as you work to bring traffic to your site.

Creating Your Own Affiliate Program (RECOMMENDED!) If on the other hand it is your chose to create your own affiliate program you have the advantage of being able to have it exactly the way you want. Just remember as your affiliate site grows and is successful your will be paying commissions to others on your sales.

This is true of our own program or one you join. This practice is a reasonable one since what you are doing is attempting to get people to your site and the more methods you have that you can use the better.

Think of it like having salespeople in your store. You would have to pay them a commission or salary to sell your goods. This is more or less the same thing.

With your affiliate site you will need to generate interest for the potential customer to come there and for others join. One way to do this is to have lots of interesting information for potential customers to read. These are usually in the form of articles.

These articles should be related to your product or service, but not all of them should be solely with the aim of selling. You will find that sometimes a less pressured sales pitch will attract more customers. Still you want to provide lots for them to read that is related to your Internet business.

Another way to bring people to your affiliate's site is make sure these articles have lots of keywords. Keywords are what the average person uses when they are searching for something on the net. For example, if a person is looking to buy a rattle for their friend's new baby, they will likely write in the words baby rattle, but they may also put in the words baby gift, new baby, baby toy etc. So, the more words that you can put in your articles that will come up in their search the more likely they will visit your site. You do not put the keywords in just once but several times so that your articles will come up nearer the top of a search. When creating your affiliates program you will want to have an interesting lead in for others to use. Pay per click is another option for you through your affiliates program. These can be highly successful but are often difficult to monitor. They can easily be abused by others to generate an income for themselves while not truly sending any traffic to your website.

Remember your affiliates program will generate your own email leads. As long as they are opt-in generated you also have the option of selling these lists. But most importantly you have them available to use along with any lists you have paid for to generate more traffic to your site as well as to help the customers who have joined your affiliate program. A common piece of advice to those who are trying to start up an affiliates program or just get an Internet business rolling is once you have discovered something that works, stay with it, then repeat it and continue your success!

Chapter 12: Leveraging on Joint Ventures

Electronic communications are the simplest way to sell your good or service today. As such, it only makes sense to continually expand your targeted email list.

But how do you go about doing this? One of the easiest ways is by networking with partners who also have email lists. However, if you are going to be effective with this, there are several things you have to keep in mind. Here are some tips on how to find partners with the tight type of email lists, and also how to use those lists to the mutual benefit of both parties.

Where To Look For Potential Partners One of the first places to check for potential partners is among professional associations. Often, you can build rapport very quickly with others who are in some way connected with the same general area of expertise that you offer with your service or product line.

Of course, you are not looking to partner with anyone who would be in direct competition with you and your company. But chances are the professional association membership will cast a wide enough net that you can find at least a few professional partners who are engaged in offering goods or services that are complimentary to what you have to offer.

As an example, let's say that you offer discounted international long distance services. You happen to belong to a professional organization for persons who are part of the telecommunications industry.

In addition to long distance, this would also include audio conferencing, web conferencing, and video conferencing. You might find it a very good fit to approach an audio conferencing provider about sharing qualified email listings. The potential for them to pick up some new conferencing customers is certainly there, and you may also find plenty of changes to snag some new corporate long distance clients as well. Along with professional associations that relate to your industry type, there are also the broader organizations, such as city and state chambers of commerce.

Membership in these types of organizations can easily pay for itself with just one good lead on someone to partner with. This will often involve making sure you attend chamber events, especially mixers.

The focus here is not necessarily to find persons who deal with services that are part of your industry, but persons whose clientele represent who new markets for you, and vice versa.

For instance, at a local chamber event, you strike up a conversation with a sales director for a national legal form supplier.

As part of their customer support, they have a monthly e-newsletter they send out to their clients. As it happens, you currently make your living selling transcription services, and have quite a few legal firms in your client base. While your two business interests may appear to not have much in common at first glance, there is plenty of reason for the two of you to talk.

You could certainly endorse the use of their forms supply business, and they in turn would be able to open doors for you to additional attorney firms, arbitration services, and others where transcriptions are key to the working day.

Trade magazines are also a great way to get leads on organizations that you may want to partner with and share email lists.

In order to do this effectively, you may want to look closely at the composition of your current client base. What industry types are represented in your base?

Which sectors of your client base are generating the most revenue for you on a monthly basis? Are there existing parts of your client base that you would like to grow?

Answers to these questions will help you determine which of the many different trade and industry magazines you want to subscribe to, and use as leads in securing venture partners.

Other Details in Joint Ventures Pay attention not only to the features, but also any columns that mention companies in passing. In like manner, see who is advertising in these magazines.

You may find some great leads among the ads. If there are classifieds in the back of the magazine, do not discount finding a good lead or two among those classifieds as well.

Of course, you do not want to forget online resources. Just about everyone is online these days in one form or another. Look for web sites that are dedicated to the type of good or service that you offer. Often, there will be links off those sites that can lead you to potential venture partners.

Many of these sites will have message boards that can also connect you with other persons who would be interested in sharing qualified email lists as part of a joint project. While these may take some time to cultivate, in the end they can provide a big payoff.

Don't forget the possibility of utilizing your own web site as a way to attract potential joint venture partners as well. Depending on your business model, it may be quite appropriate to create a page that is meant to attract potential partners in a join email sharing campaign. Provide some basic guidelines that have to be met, such as proof that the list is qualified, that it is a current and usable list, and that no one is included without express permission. Then provide a way for anyone interested to contact you about moving forward. It cannot be stressed enough that you make sure to only work with persons who can provide a legitimate email list of persons who have requested to receive email transmissions.

There are far too many email lists on sale these days that are antiquated or compiled from sources that would do nothing to help you reach your target audience.

Whether you meet a potential joint venture partner face to face at a chamber event, or make your first contact via a message board or a response to a query on your web site, you must set the standard.

Important JV Tip:

Make sure that you only deal with people who have the same level of ethics and respect for potential clients that you have worked long and hard to cultivate and establish.

Failure to do so will mean lost time and resources, few if any new clients, and most likely loss of some of your clients as well. Pick your partners carefully, however, and you will open up all sorts of opportunities to broaden your client base and increase your revenue stream.

Chapter 13: Executing Product Launches

As any good businessperson knows, nothing is quite as exciting as launching a new product or service. One of the best ways to have your new offering hit the ground running is by using a resource you already have in place to get the word out to interested parties: your customer email list.

Product Launch For Hard Hitters Utilization of your email list should begin long before the actual launch date of the new product or service. A savvy approach is to begin using the electronic communications to begin building up some interest in the new product.

As an example, let's assume that you do a monthly newsletter to your client list. Several months before the launch start inserting teasers into the newsletter.

Even something simple like "Not sure what to get your best friend for Christmas this year?

In September, we will tell you." Of course, you may want to be more direct and try something along the lines of "You told us you want it.

And we listened. Announcing EasyWeb, our new web conferencing product, coming in August."

Of course, every month you will include a new tidbit about the new offering.

Use the space to extol the advantages of your offering over those from your competition.

Along with the teasers, build up to a feature article that goes into the background on how the product was developed and what influence existing customers had on the final design.

Customers love to know you listen, even if many of them never send you any ideas.

Pre-Launch:

As the time for the launch draws near, you may want to do some promotional work among your email listing as well. Offer premiums such as discounts to any existing client that can get someone who is not currently a customer to attend a demonstration of the product and who subsequently signs up for the product or service.

Among your client base, why not offer a short-term free trial, as well.

The point is to give your existing clients a chance to try your new offering, decide that they like it, and that they will be coming back for more.

Happy customers are some of the best word of mouth you will ever have, so if they like you and your new offering, they will be more than happy to promote you to other organizations.

In addition to using your regular e-newsletter to publicize the advent of your new offering, you may also want to do targeted emails from your email list.

Targeted emails would involve dividing your email list up according to industry type and preparing the text of an email that would point to applications of your new offering that are of special interest to that part of your client base.

As an example, you may have a large percentage of non-profit associations in your client base. You know that your new offering could help them keep track of participation in fund raising projects they conduct.

Focus on that point, explaining how your offering can make the job easier and more accurate.

Critical Launch Success Factors:

It is important to note that you will not get a very good response if you do not do two things. First, you must send several well-timed emails about your offering between the time you make the first announcement and the actual launch date. Far too many people think that one announcement does the trick and there is nothing more to be done.

The fact is the matter is that you want to use your email list to build interest for your offering as the launch date approaches. Depending on your client base, a monthly email might be just fine. If you think you can do so more often, than give it a try.

You want to keep people informed, give them ideas on how to use your offering, but you do not want them to get tired of seeing emails from you and decide to opt out of your list. Find that sweet spot for contacts and you will be able to use the list effectively.

Also, it is not a matter of using material versus sending out individual emails. By all means use both. Chances are that your clients will take note of one or the other, but not necessarily both forms of electronic communication.

Of course, you want the emails and the newsletter content to compliment one another.

In fact, you may want the text of your email to refer back to the content in the newsletter, and vice versa. Keep everything consistent and very upbeat.

Along with getting out information on the potential applications of your offering, you may want to invite your client base to participate in some sort of a contest, with the prize being something that would be useful in the home or office.
However you choose to construct the contest you need to make sure of two things. First, it is imperative that you be able to verify the results.

Secondly, you should offer a prize that will not create any undue hardship on your company. You want it to be attractive, but not something that will potentially create a situation where you would not be able to meet your obligations. Of course it makes sense to only offer a three-day, two-night cruise to the winner if you can afford to do so.

Launching Your Product:

Don't forget to follow up the launch date with some more updates and invitations to try out the new offering. Continue to spotlight the launched service or product in your e-newsletter and in email communiqués to your client for at least four to six months after the launch.

The potential for them to share your announcements and feature reports with other people will not end on the day of the launch. Keep the momentum going and you may pick up a few more customers.

Your email list is a valuable piece of property. It is important that you responsibly use it to keep your current customers happy with you and your offerings, as well as let them know of new innovations that can make life easier for them.

At the same, time, it can be a wonderful way to involve your clients in the process of securing new customers who can benefit from a working relationship with you. Make sure your customers always know how much you appreciate them and you will be able to not only maintain but also continue to expand your email list every time you have something new to offer.

Maximizing Your Mailing List Profit Points:

Having a solid mailing list is one of your business' greatest assets.

Many of us know that the single most powerful selling tool we have is the good word of mouth we get from our existing customers. The fact of the matter is that your customers can help you to grow your business in several ways, as you find ways to up-sell them on other means of helping you help them grow their business.

Here are some suggestions that will help you articulate to your customers how you can help them grow while you are maximizing the profits that you get from your mailing list and e-zines.

Sell Advertising Space To Your Clients:

Chances are that at least some of your clients are involved in selling goods and services that would be of interest to other customers on your mailing list. So what if you were to offer some really competitive advertising space in your monthly electronic magazine?

This one simple offer could begin a whole new revenue stream for you, using a resource that at present does not provide any direct profit. In order to keep things as simple as possible, you could specify the format of the ad and also offer sizes that would be very easy to include, such as quarter page, half page and page size advertisements.
Just as with any ad service, you could offer short term and long term rates for advertising in the newsletter, which would mean a steady revenue stream for you over the long term. Along with the newsletter, have you thought about offering the contacts in your email list the ability to place ads with hot links on your web site? You could create a whole section of advertising that is just for your client base. As for pricing, you could set up a basic monthly rate, and offer discounts off that for commitments of six months, a year, or two years of advertising via your web site.

Assuming that you send invoices through regular mail, you could also create a lucrative revenue stream by advertising to contacts on your email list the ability to include advertising flyers in all your mailings.

Of course, you would want to pieces to fit nicely into standard business envelope and you would want to make sure you kept the number of inserts to a minimum. Nevertheless, you could create a steady flow of cash from even this type of endeavor.

Another form of advertising you could offer to your clientele is to include a onetime feature article in your monthly E-zine.

The article could include an overview of the history of the company, vital information about their core product line, or information about an upcoming new good or service they will be launching soon.

This feature article option could be offered with a guaranteed minimum word count as well as a bold header, for a flat rate price. Of course, you could also offer a sliding scale based on a fixed rate per word instead of the flat fee. This would allow your client to opt for a longer article, if they wish to do so.

Affiliate Programs And Your Email List:

The simple fact of the matter is that no one is successful with an affiliate program without owning a good solid email list. Since you already have a list that meets those qualifications, why not put your email list to work and make some money with affiliate programs?

Here Is What You Need To Do:

The genius of opting into an affiliate program is that you get to expand the types of goods and services that you offer to your existing customer base without having to invest anything into development, facilities, or production.

Someone else has already done all of that. By entering into an affiliate agreement, you tap into that resource, act at the mediator, and rake in profit off every unit sold.

One of the first things you will need to do is collect data on available affiliate programs. A quick Internet search will probably lead you to quite a number of potential programs that would be of interest to you.
You may also uncover a source or two that will provide you with quick overviews of hundreds of affiliate programs that are actively looking for persons just like you.

Make notes of anything and everything that you think could possibly be of interest to you. One thing to note here is that you will be able to find plenty of affiliate programs that will work just fine with your own sense of business ethics.

While there may be some programs out there that offer products that you would prefer to not be connected with, do not worry about limiting yourself. The breadth and depth of affiliate programs is such that you will have no problem finding plenty to chose from. After you have made your initial swing through the lists, is it time to begin matching up your interests and skill sets with what you understand about your own clientele.

As you look at each of the affiliate programs that have caught your eye, think in terms of what your customers do for a living. What products or services would be likely to compliment what you already sell, or at least be of some interest to those that already know and do business with you?

You can sign up for all sorts of affiliate programs, but if they are not going to excite those who already know you, then what is the point? Make sure that any affiliate program you sign up with has the potential to generate additional income from your email list.

Next, you want to do some checking on any affiliate program that you are sure is a good fit for you and the customers on your existing email list. What will you be looking for?

Find evidence that the program is stable, that it delivers what it promises, and that the majority of the folks who are affiliates are happy with the way things are going. Where will you find this information? On the Internet, of course.

Use your Internet browser to conduct a search for comments on the affiliate program of your choice. You want to locate as much feedback, both positive and negative, as you can manage.

No organization is going to be without its detractors, so don't let some negative comments turn you off immediately. How well an organization responds to the need to resolve an issue with an unhappy client says as much about it as having customers who do not experience problems.

What you do want to be aware of are any trends that indicate the affiliate program is misleading in some way, that it fails to live up to its promises, and that it consistently has a history of leaving affiliates in the lurch.
When you find ample evidence of that sort of behavior, then you know it is time to forget about that program and move on to the next one on your list.

Once you have identified one or more affiliate programs that you feel good about representing, then the next move is to let the folks on your email list know what is going on. Prepare a press release announcing your decision to open a working relationship with your new partner.

Outline some of the reasons why you have decided that these affiliates are a good match for what you already provide to your customers. You may want to include some bullets that demonstrate some reasons why your customers should look at your new partner(s) very closely.

Make sure that you have a link set up on your web site that will function as a portal to your new partner(s), so you can get credit for any business your clients do with any of your partners is credited to you.

If you have an E-zine that you produce on a regular basis, promote the products of your partners right along with your own services.

Keep the name of your affiliate partner(s) in front of your customers through the use of both email and your E-zine, as well as making sure there is a link to your partner on your web site.

Along with opening up new revenue streams by using your email list to promote this new affiliate relationship, you also can make sure that your existing customers have the means to pass on your information to their associates.

This can lead to the expansion of your opt-in email listing, additional demand for your own services, and increase revenue from your affiliate relationship as well.

Always Remember To Market Your Own Services One of the reasons you have such a great email list in the first place is that people have come to know you and trust you. You've sold them goods and services before, and they have liked what they got both in the way of product and in the way of customer care.

Your job is to not only maintain that positive relationship, but also to build upon it. Upselling is the term that is normally used for the process of promoting goods and services to your existing clientele that they have not yet tried out. In many ways, this is much easier than trying to start with a new lead. There is already a history between you and the buyer, one that has demonstrated a good working relationship up to that point.

Chances are that your client will at least devote a few minutes to whatever new product or service that you want to introduce them to. It is your job to use the resources at hand to make sure that courtesy of giving you a few moments turns into a sale.

When it comes to email announcements, make them big and broad, but keep in mind that not all people utilize HTML setting for their inbound email.

For that reason, you may want to rely more heavily on the content and less of using graphics to spotlight a new or existing service.

In order to get the most our of your email announcement content, you will want to observe a few basic rules.
First, make sure that the content of the email announcement is focused. Do not try to cover too much ground at one time.

Keep the content in line with the purpose of the email, which is to promote one particular product in your line.

If availability is pending, make that clear right up front, including the date that the product will be available. Outline at least three possible applications of the product that, based on your knowledge of your customer base, will appeal to a majority of them. Close with contact information to learn more about the product, including a link back to the page on your web site that features the product.

Second, make your email announcement can be easily scanned by your audience. Many people will glance over your email and then move on.

You can diminish that occurrence by having the announcement broken down so that key points will catch the eye of even the most casual reader and impel him or her to go back to the beginning and read all the way through.

Using headers and bullets are an effective way to make your announcement more scanner friendly, and will help hold the attention of the reader.

Last, make sure the email announcement is simply that: an announcement. The communication is not meant to function as a sales brochure, nor is it supposed to be an exhaustive study of the new product. It is meant to spark the interest of the reader and provide them with just enough detail to compel them to want more information. Generally speaking, if you can keep the announcement under 500 words, you will manage to keep the attention of your audience long enough to make your point.

In Conclusion... As the last section of the series in the Ultimate List Builders Course draws to an end, remember: your email listing can help you to generate additional AND substantial ongoing revenue for your Online Business. By offering advertising space on your web site and in your E-zine, you provide customers with the chance to reach a whole new audience, one that already trusts you to steer them in the right direction.

The use of affiliate programs creates opportunities to build on the relationships you already have with everyone who has opted into receiving electronic communications from you by offering them a wider range of products and services. Last, your email list provides you with a bank of persons who are already receptive to doing business with you, and will often be very happy to know about any new goods or services you are offering to them. With each of these three examples, and especially if you allow them to overlap in the way you utilize your email list, you have the opportunity to greatly expand your revenue stream, as well as broaden your client base.

To Your Ultimate Mastery Of List Building & The Maximizing Of Your Profits!

To Your Complete Success!

Resources:

Besides the links throughout the course, there are a few other favorite resources I'd like to share with you. I've used them myself and so I can confidently recommend them to you for your business.

Marketing & Business Tools You'll Need:

Payment Processor:
2CheckOut is my favorite

ClickBank is only for digital products but is good, too PayPal is a good free alternative to get started out Hosting:

Hostgator is a place for hosting multiple domains very affordably.

Domain Name Registrar:

Ifastnet.com offers excellent service & pricing plus some other extras you may need besides your domain names.

Autoresponders:

All of these are good solid (and necessary) products...

Aweber
GetResponse
ListMailPro
FollowUpExpert:
MyAutoresponderPro

My Favorite List-Building Resources:
ClickFunnels
Nitro List Builder
List-Opt's List Builder

Awesome Membership Site Script:

Amember works great for an affordable, easy member site script!

Positive reviews from awesome customers like you help others to feel confident about choosing this book. Thanks very much !

The End - (BONUS 3) Free Book : "Email List Building"

By : "Santiago Johnson Smith"

DISCLAIMER AND TERMS OF USE AGREEMENT:

The author and publisher of this course and the accompanying materials have used their best efforts in preparing this course. The author and publisher make no representation or warranties with respect to the accuracy, applicability, fitness, or completeness of the contents of this course. The information contained in this course is strictly for educational purposes. Therefore, if you wish to apply ideas contained in this course, you are taking full responsibility for your actions.

Every effort has been made to accurately represent this product and it's potential. Even though this industry is one of the few where one can write their own check in terms of earnings, there is no guarantee that you will earn any money using the techniques and ideas in these materials. Examples in these materials are not to be interpreted as a promise or guarantee of earnings.

Continue to the next page...

Forward-looking statements give our expectations or forecasts of future events. you can identify these statements by the fact that they do not relate strictly to historical or current facts. They use words such as "anticipate," "estimate," "expect," "project," "intend," "plan," "believe," and other words and terms of similar meaning in connection with a description of potential earnings or financial performance. Any and all forward looking statements here or on any of our sales material are intended to express our opinion of earnings potential. Many factors will be important in determining your actual results and no guarantees are made that you will achieve results similar to ours or anybody elses, in fact no guarantees are made that you will achieve any results from our ideas and techniques in our material.

The author and publisher disclaim any warranties (express or implied), merchantability, or fitness for any particular purpose. The author and publisher shall in no event be held liable to any party for any direct, indirect, punitive, special, incidental or other consequential damages arising directly or indirectly from any use of this material, which is provided "as is", and without warranties. As always, the advice of a competent legal, tax, accounting or other professional should be sought. The author and publisher do not warrant the performance, effectiveness or applicability of any sites listed or linked to in this course. All links are for information purposes only and are not warranted for content, accuracy or any other implied or explicit purpose.